From Scratch and on a Shoestring

How absolutely anyone can build an outstanding practice

By Arthur A. Leidecker, BCH, CI

With Foreword By

The Reverend C. Scot Giles, D.Min.

LifeStrategies Publishing
273 E. Chicago Street
Elgin, Illinois 60120
lifestrtgy@aol.com

LifeStrategies Publishing,
273 E. Chicago Street,
Elgin, IL 60120.

Note for Librarians: A cataloguing record for this book is available from Library and Archives Canada at www.collectionscanada.ca/amicus/index-e.html
ISBN 1-55212-972-1

First printing November, 2001.

Printed in Victoria, BC, Canada. Printed on paper with minimum 30% recycled fibre. Trafford's print shop runs on "green energy" from solar, wind and other environmentally-friendly power sources.

TRAFFORD
PUBLISHING™
Offices in Canada, USA, Ireland and UK

Book sales for North America and international:
Trafford Publishing, 6E–2333 Government St.,
Victoria, BC V8T 4P4 CANADA
phone 250 383 6864 (toll-free 1 888 232 4444)
fax 250 383 6804; email to orders@trafford.com
Book sales in Europe:
Trafford Publishing (UK) Limited, 9 Park End Street, 2nd Floor
Oxford, UK OX1 1HH UNITED KINGDOM
phone 44 (0)1865 722 113 (local rate 0845 230 9601)
facsimile 44 (0)1865 722 868; info.uk@trafford.com
Order online at:
trafford.com/01-0374

10 9 8 7 6 5 4

To
my patient wife Marilyn who never gives up.

Table of Contents

Foreword

By The Reverend C. Scot Giles, D. Min.

This is an important book. Over the years many people have come to me and asked for advice on how to set up and run a successful practice as helping professionals. They come because I have a thriving practice and they wish to have one too. It has been a great source of frustration to me that up until now there has been no textbook to recommend that would lay out a reliable strategy for success.

Arthur Leidecker does the professional community a great service by drawing together in this book the best advice of marketing professionals gathered in his many years of lucrative business life, and combines it with his own sensitive observations gathered over a lifetime as a world traveler. What he teaches here can be trusted. I have known him for many years and can testify that he is successful, ethical and knows more about business than I ever shall.

More than a decade ago I opened my own hypnotherapy practice. During the first difficult years I made many expensive mistakes. If I had this book available to me I would have avoided those mistakes. Looking back over those years I clearly see that the techniques that worked best for me, discovered through laborious trial and error, were basically the techniques Art Leidecker recommends here. I even learned some new techniques by reading the manuscript for this book.

We live in a time when alternative and complementary health care is on the rise. Each year more and more practitioners enter the marketplace. It is in the best interests of all of us that these practitioners succeed, for successful practitioners create satisfied clients who tell their friends. This creates an expanding market for our services and will bring abundance to us all. This book is a great contribution to that future.

Wheaton, Illinois
2001

The Rev. Dr. C. Scot Giles is a psychiatric chaplain and the director of the Wheaton Regional Office of Counseling Ministries, a Chicago-area ecumenical group pastoral counseling and care organization. Dr. Giles holds two degrees in Philosophy from the University of Connecticut and his Doctor of Ministry degree from Meadville/Lombard Theological School at the University of Chicago. He is a Board Certified Chaplain with the Association of Mental Health Clergy, an affiliate of the American Psychiatric Association and a member of the Congress on Ministry in Specialized Settings. Dr. Giles also is a National Guild of Hypnotists' Board Certified Hypnotherapist.

Acknowledgements

I am grateful to the practitioners of complementary healing modalities that have strived for true professionalism, and persevered in the midst of a changing world of healing and health care. Their personal professional efforts are clearing pathways often filled with obstacles resistant to change.

Because there's no medical system, or rarely any insurance payment to support them, they must market their services well to survive as well as earn respect for their profession.

I would also like to give acknowledgement to The Economics Press Inc., the publisher of *Bits And Pieces,* a great little book of quotes and inspirations that come to me regularly in the mail. They've been motivating readers around the world for over 30 years. On days I've felt less than motivated, a few minutes spent browsing through my current copy always got me back on track.

I would also like to thank all my students and clients. Their response to my marketing techniques and their feedback through surveys and course evaluations have helped me develop the marketing strategies that worked best to attract the caliber of clients and students I was looking for.

And last but not least, my friends that favored me with their peer review, and my hardworking wife, Marilyn, who reread this book seven times while editing and proofreading it.

Preface

Elephants And Fleas

This is a book for ambitious people. You'll find many things written that at first glance may not seem to apply to your business or practice in particular. But don't let anything slip past you. The ability to identify things that can be used or integrated from one business or practice into another is a strong characteristic of many very successful entrepreneurs. Make a habit after you've finished this book, to always keep your eyes open to the possibility of using something from another profession or business, making the necessary adjustments to integrate it into yours.

José Silva, the originator of the world famous *Silva Mind Control* program, once said to me, "The mind is like a parachute—it works best when it's open."

My goal is to provide you with a multitude of systems, procedures, and ideas that you can put to work immediately. By the time you've applied half of what you read here, you'll be so busy with clients, patients, or customers, that it will become difficult to apply the second half of the strategies.

I've researched marketing styles all over the world—even sales by children. The Kurdish children in Turkey have become masters at their favorite techniques. Egyptian children selling souvenirs at the pyramids are master salespeople using proxemics that most Westerners are not even aware of. I interviewed a top hypnotherapist in Ireland that continuously bills over a million pounds a year using his favorite marketing strategy. From China to South America I've witnessed everyone marketing in their favorite way. They all do what works for them but most only use one favorite strategy. Once they've found something that worked, their search was over. While these people are all succeeding, you'll want to apply several strategies and create multiple streams of income.

A graduate student called me and asked for a favor. He wanted me to write an ad for him. "Not an ordinary ad, but one that will bring me twenty clients a week." I first explained that I don't intentionally write two kinds of ads— "ordinary," and good. Also, that while I couldn't write him an affordable ad that would bring twenty clients, I could give him twenty ideas that would each bring a client. And that's what it takes—a lot of different strategies applied in different ways at different times. If you only work one or two good marketing strategies, you'll be doing what everyone else does. It's always been my belief that: **if you do what everyone else does, you'll have to settle for what everyone else gets.** I always wanted more. By making a commitment to do more, success was assured. **Success is a decision—not good fortune.**

"Your IQ is not as important as your
"I WILL."

Author Unknown

Out of the clear blue sky one day, a friend said to me, "You're not really successful because you're smart Art, you just keep trying different things." When it comes down to it, I guess he's right. However, he's got the smarts—I've got the money.

Have you noticed that often someone that's experienced fabulous success goes broke through some misfortune, and before you know it they're up and running again? Why is that? Fear—they have none. They've figured it out! No one's going to grind you up and eat you if you fail. In fact, they don't even consider it failure. They chalk it up to learning. If a venture doesn't work out, and you quit trying—that's failure. But if you don't give up, and try again, it's learning.

Once someone has made it to the top, even if they lose it all, they can get back up quickly again because they no longer have the fear of failure—they've already faced it. They've also cast aside all their self-limiting beliefs.

"When you go to bat as many times as I do, you're bound to get a good average."
Walt Disney (1901—1966)
                                    Film Entrepreneur

Elephants are led around by men and women that don't weigh as much as their trunks. The ropes that hold them are so thin that they could break them with just the turn of their head. How is it that they don't break loose? It's self-limiting belief. When baby elephants are first tethered, it only takes a light cord to hold them. As they grow, they don't pull hard enough against the cord to break it because they still believe it can hold them. As soon as they feel the resistance from the cord, their belief causes them to stop pulling. Eventually they grow to the size that makes them strong enough to tow a truck, but their self-limiting belief keeps them controlled by the cord that "holds" them.

Back a few years ago, some researchers wanted to see how long it would take for fleas to learn that they couldn't jump out of a large jar. They put a number of fleas in a jar with holes in the lid and began charting how long they kept trying to jump out. You probably guessed it, they never gave up— they just kept on jumping. Next, they tried taking the lid off. You probably guessed it again. The fleas only jumped as high as they thought they could, because they were limited by the belief that they couldn't jump any higher.

4

Once the four-minute mile was finally run, it became a feat accomplished by many since it was no longer believed that it couldn't be done. It was the same with scaling Mt. Everest, and so many other challenges.

Many professionals and business people are of the mind that they shouldn't have to market their practice, or think they can just put ads in the papers and the people will come. That way of doing business is in the past by fifty years. Even medical doctors find they need to market today. I've had students tell me they just want to do hypnotherapy, that they're not really into marketing. My answer to them is that the hypnotherapy is the fun part that you get to do after doing a good job of marketing.

I've seen good chiropractors close up shop because they couldn't make it, while others were extremely busy all the time. I trained a psychotherapist that had so much business that he refused to take any insurance cases because he didn't want to fool with forms. He marketed his practice so well that he didn't have to. His clients all paid cash out of pocket.

When I conduct my marketing workshops, many attendees are just about to set out on their own. I always ask them to honestly rate their performance at their current job. If they rate it poorly, or mediocre, I ask them why. The usual answer is that they hate their job. The truth is: if you do poorly because you hate your job, you'd best look at your ability to discipline yourself. Because in your own business, you'll find a lot of tasks you'll not like, and in the beginning you may not have anyone to relegate them to. **The decision to be successful is yours alone. Undeveloped individuals always look for success outside of themselves.** Be prepared to rely on the one person that you can count on—you.

*For ease of reading, I have used the generic *he* throughout this book.

Introduction

It wasn't my feet sweating from the plastic imitation leather shoes that got to me; it was the way they froze as soon as I went back outside on the cold winter days. I often half-jokingly told myself that they were a great motivator. If I stayed on a sales call too long my feet sweated. If I stayed on the street too long they froze. The best solution was to make as many sales calls as I could. I only persisted because I was convinced at that time that airfreight sales offered me a great opportunity.

By this time I was forty-three years old and rebuilding for a third time after taking devastating, undeserved losses.

I think my story is important because it shows just how tough it can get before you finally get a break. But no matter how tough it gets, if you're determined, you'll learn enough along the way to reach your goals.

I like the analogy of a tomato plant. When at first you plant a tomato seed in an indoor planter, it comes up very quickly. It is, however, like a very thin strand of thread. If you were to plant it outside, either the sun would immediately burn it up, or the rain would beat it into the ground. It must first be toughened. The way that's done is to put it out night after night in the cold. The cold toughens it and the thin stem becomes thicker and strong. Once it's had enough exposure to the cold, it's ready to go into the ground.

That's pretty much how we are. If we can't weather a little cold, we're not cut out for operating our own enterprise and need to go back into the shelter of a job.

By the age of thirty I had six real estate offices, nineteen buildings, a gas station, carwash, farm, and a new home. I was enjoying a great lifestyle with a very promising future. I won't put myself through the agony of what happened again by describing all the events in detail, but I learned to work every day at staying positive and letting go of what had happened to me, not once, but twice.

I'll get back to the airfreight sales later—it's key to my story.

When I was five years old, I picked all the rhubarb from a patch, threw it in my wagon, and went off down the street selling rhubarb for five cents a bunch. Sales were brisk. I don't know if the demand for rhubarb was that great, or if people were just getting a kick out of me. I found that if I went into the hallway of apartment buildings and rang all the bells at one time, I would create a lot of activity and got a lot of attention. No more single residences for me. I only went to a few more apartment buildings and I was sold out.

Unfortunately, when I got home and my mother found out I had picked all the neighbors rhubarb, she insisted that I turn all the proceeds over to him. He didn't want the money but my mother wouldn't have it any other way. I wasn't punished. If I had been, who knows? It may have snuffed out my entrepreneurial spark for good.

I'm starting out with my story because I learned some very valuable lessons—the hard way.

You may have already learned some, or even most. But even if you have, you'll be all the more appreciative of a chance to learn one or two here rather than on your own. Read my story cafeteria style: take what you like, pass on the rest.

Money was tight when I was very young. My father had a habit of abandoning my mom and I for weeks at a time with no food or money. Later a baby sister came along and joined us in our suffering. We learned to hate peanut butter on whole wheat bread with homemade pea soup, but it sustained us until I was old enough to baby-sit my younger sister and my mom could get a job. Shortly after, mom got a lawyer, the locks were changed, and papers were served.

I've been told some people are born hardheaded. I believe it. At least my mother's new husband was. But life was so much better. He actually came home every night, and on Fridays he brought home his un-cashed paycheck. But he was hardheaded. By the time I was fifteen, my new dad had forbidden me to get on anyone's motorbike, and no, I couldn't ever buy one, so there was no sense in even beginning to save for one. By this time I had already been working five to eight hours a day after school at a gas station and auto repair shop that I remained at until I was almost twenty-one.

Although I couldn't have a motorbike, he never said I couldn't have a car. I found a way. After my regular job, I worked at a late night gas station in exchange for a used car my boss had for sale. I couldn't drive it, but I owned it—for a year before I could drive. By the time I was sixteen, it had been polished and tuned up so many times it looked and ran like new.

My family didn't own a car. We used to stand at the bus stop waiting in the cold, across the street from my car parked at the gas station. I wasn't old enough to drive it, and my dad wouldn't even acknowledge the fact that it was sitting there unused. So we stood in the cold at the bus stop all winter whenever the family went somewhere. Finally, just before I turned sixteen and got my driver's license, my dad hurried out and bought a car. A week later we had two cars in front of the house.

I began buying older cars, fixing and selling them. The profits were good, but I wanted more. I was saving three fourths of every dollar I made from my salary at the auto shop and thought that if I made money fixing cars, I should be able to make money buying and fixing houses. At sixteen I bought two waterfront lots in a lake area not too far from home. I thought maybe I would start out by building a home to sell. (My mom had to sign the contract for the lots.)

I got an education in real estate quickly. After I bought the lots I found out they weren't buildable. So I sold them to an attorney, who a few years later became a business partner.

When I turned eighteen I bought my first home. It was a resort area summer cottage, which I bought for ten thousand dollars. (In 1958 that was a lot of money for a kid.) After insulating it and installing a used furnace that I bought cheap, I sold it for fifteen thousand dollars. A cool fifty percent profit. This was certainly better than the cars that I was still fixing and selling on the side while working in the gas station/auto shop.

When I started working at the gas station at age thirteen, my boss told me that if I worked hard, one day I could become a partner in the business—I believed that. It was always the carrot held out in front of me. After working what amounted to almost half of my young lifetime at that job, I approached him when I reached the age of twenty to make our "partnership" deal. He told me that I couldn't afford to buy half because it would take at least five thousand dollars (a lot of money in 1959). I told him I had the money and was ready. He then told me the truth. He didn't want to, and wasn't going to. That was another tough life-lesson. Lesson learned:

Life doesn't have to be fair.

I packed my tools and was gone the same day. I didn't realize it at the time, but my greedy boss did me a big favor. I decided that I had worked under the hoods of cars long enough and was ready for real estate. I sold my tools and went to work at a real estate company. Shortly after, I bought in as a partner and then expanded the business to six offices.

Then the "life doesn't have to be fair," thing happened again. I received a heavy bundle of papers with a heading that changed my life. "The United States of America vs. Arthur A. Leidecker." It appeared that due to a full-page story about me written by a major Chicago daily newspaper, a lot of attention was brought to my success. I had been advertising apartment rentals heavily, and the newspapers were classifying the ads geographically by street boundaries. Whenever the ads were called in to the ad-takers, we gave the location descriptions according to the boundaries set by the newspaper. If we did not give them in accordance with

11

these boundaries, the newspaper either corrected them and put them in the right classification, or just rejected the ad. To operate efficiently, we memorized and adhered to the newspapers' mandatory boundaries.

The Justice Department decided that this was racial discrimination and filed a "discrimination through advertising" lawsuit against me. I wasn't worried. I knew that this was a mistake and that surely they would correct it and take the issue up with the newspaper, since they had created the boundaries and required that I adhere to them. To my surprise, my response fell on deaf ears. They had a consent decree for me to sign in lieu of going to trial. The problem with the consent decree was that there was no way I could continue to do business while complying with it. My impression was that you were innocent until proven guilty of something, so what was there to fear?

I brought my bundle of papers to my attorneys who explained to me that even though I was very successful, I didn't have enough money to take on the United States of America. I told them I didn't want to take on the United States; I just wanted to defend myself. The burden of proof was on them. Since I was innocent, they couldn't prove me guilty of anything. After patiently explaining to me how it *really* works, and how costly it would be to defend myself, I finally took their advice, went out of business, and dropped out of real estate. Lesson learned:
                              Life doesn't have to be fair.

You might think "Well he still had the gas station and car wash," right? Do you remember the stories about the oil crisis of 1972? You probably guessed it. I couldn't get enough gas to operate my station.

12

I sold it at a loss. The man that bought it lost even more than I did.

Still, I had the real estate properties. As luck would have it, I had a devastating fire in a fully paid for, nineteen flat building. My insurance broker friend was on a California junket when my insurance company had notified him that they were not renewing my policy—he forgot to notify me. The loss was totally mine. I apologized to him for having to do it, but I had no choice but to file a claim against his errors and omissions policy. Would you believe he only carried five thousand dollars worth? And, it was with a thousand dollars deductible at that. He gave me the check to cover his thousand along with the four thousand from the insurance company—hardly enough to cover the loss. Then his check was returned by the bank. He had stopped payment. He had no intentions of paying me his share. Lesson learned:

Life doesn't have to be fair.

"The gem cannot be polished without friction, nor man perfected without trials."

Confucius (551—479 B.C.)
Philosopher

Having lost almost everything, I looked over opportunities for a period of time and settled on the airfreight industry. This was mainly because many of the people that I had met in this business seemed rather unsophisticated, yet they were quite successful. I saw it as a good opportunity—I knew that if they were successful, all I had to do was watch what they did, do it better, and do more of it, and I would be even more successful than them. That was my game plan—nothing more, nothing less.

"Most people work just hard enough to not get fired and get paid just enough money not to quit."

George Carlin
Comedian

Do What Everyone Else Does — Get What Everyone Else Gets

My first airfreight sales job was tough to get. Everyone wanted salesmen with airfreight sales experience. The only way I could break in was to work cheap, and work well. I set out to do more than my contemporaries. Soon I realized that most airfreight salesmen weren't working very hard.

> *"Many people are like a wheelbarrow—they go on no further than they are pushed."*
>
> Bits and Pieces

It was easy to make a good showing, and I was soon offered a better job for much more money and benefits. Then it became time to be reminded of my continuously repeating lesson. Just as I was getting back on my feet, I got a notice from the IRS requesting my presence.

They were claiming that I owed them an incredible amount of money from my previous business. I was able to determine that they had made a huge mistake, and that I didn't owe them after all. Much to my surprise, when I showed the IRS agent their error, she disagreed with me, slapped a lien on our home, confiscated our paychecks and savings, and informed me that our home would be put up for sale in a tax auction in thirty days. You already know the lesson:

Life doesn't have to be fair.

There was no time to do anything. I had a difficult time borrowing money because all my checks I had written to pay my mortgage and bills had just bounced due to the IRS confiscating my checking account funds. I didn't even have grocery money—they took it. I had to scour the house for treasures that I could live without to sell for grocery and utility money. Finally, I found a sympathetic loan agent at one of those friendly convenient loan companies that put a second mortgage on our home in exchange for a high interest loan. Naturally, the loan check was made out to the IRS to be sure I paid the bill.

To add a little more stress to the situation, a very good friend of mine had just filed for divorce and served his wife notice—about two hours before he found out he needed back surgery and couldn't work at his job any more. So now we also had a boarder—a free one.

"Adversity has the effect of eliciting talents, which, in prosperous circumstances, would have lain dormant."

Horace (65—8 B.C.)
Poet and Satirist

With a family of five to support, this called for a good game plan.

"Opportunity's favorite disguise is trouble."

Frank Tyger

16

I got rid of our second car and started driving my wife to and from work every day. We both quit smoking. I became a skilled grocery shopper and budget cook, and found every way possible to legally and honestly beat the system.

I found that if I bought the lunch meat and cheese ends at the supermarket, I could put them in French bread with a little olive oil, wrap them in foil, and heat them in the oven as hot "oven grinder" sandwiches. They were great! I could make them up in batches and freeze them. No two were alike. They, along with pasta and bean dishes and occasional meat from a sale, became the staples of our diet.

Eventually we adjusted to our austere lifestyle, and life became somewhat bearable. The IRS was paid, but now we had the whopping loan to pay back. I earned a few raises during the next year, and life looked as if it would still go on. The IRS never removed the liens they had put against our home, but I didn't have the money to hire an attorney to straighten that out. In the meantime, I was learning a little about the airfreight business, and developing several sales strategies and techniques of my own that really worked well. Then came a new lesson:

Work hard and you sometimes get a break!

One day I stopped home for a minute and grabbed the mail on the way into the house. Lo and behold there was a whopping check in the mail from the IRS. It was almost all the money I had paid them—almost a year and a half later. No explanatory letter—just a whopping check! I really deserved an apology, and the amount was not one hundred percent correct; but I didn't want to talk with them, nor did I want any contact with them whatsoever. I deposited my "refund" and went on my way. Lesson learned:

Let sleeping dogs lie.

"Success is going from failure to failure without loss of enthusiasm."
Winston Churchill (1874—1965)
British Prime Minister

After a sum total of four years of airfreight experience, I began getting restless. I knew that if I was going to make up for lost time I was going to have to put my mind to work in better ways. You can only move your hands so fast and so much in one day. I've always believed that a brain surgeon is limited by how fast and skillfully he can move his hands. He can only perform so many surgeries a day. But a person using their mind closer to its capacity, can create unlimited wealth. Your mind can move faster than your hands. It later gave me a feeling of extreme satisfaction to go to the doctor or dentist knowing I was making far more money than he ever dreamed of making.

I set out to prove my theory. Every morning for several months, I spent fifteen or twenty minutes doing self-hypnosis while in my car, before making my first sales call. I used a simple process that I was taught by a hypnotist.

I closed my eyes and imagined myself going down in a custom, private elevator. Floor by floor, I slowly counted my way down to a deeply relaxed state. When I finally reached the first floor, I would open the doors and enter a wonderful garden where I could relax and focus my concentration.

I visualized myself as being very successful and accumulating wealth. I gave myself post-hypnotic suggestions that I was wealthy and successful. I believed it was happening, and I was preparing myself for it—knowing it was going to happen. I went about my business doing my job, and then the day I was preparing my subconscious for arrived. An idea popped into my head that made millions.

"The value in an idea lies in the using of it."
Thomas Edison
(1847—1931)
Inventor

When the idea popped, I knew it was good. So good that it supported my long time belief that if any idea is truly good, it won't take any big money to get it off the ground. Airfreight salesmen were a dime a dozen. I had to be different—I had to come up with something unique that hadn't been done before.

I had ten dollars worth of business cards printed, calling myself a "Transportation Consultant." I then made a sales call on Paramount Pictures while they had a booth at the electronics show in Chicago. I knew that they were having trouble with their distribution of movie title releases on video. Home video was a new industry. This was in the days of the video clubs when the videocassettes were not yet for sale in discount chains. You could only rent them or buy them from video stores.

A major movie company had just finished releasing *Star Wars* on video and was disappointed in the sales. Paramount had announced that they were releasing their big title *Star Trek Two, The Wrath Of Kahn*, the next month and they were on a course headed for the same disappointment. The problem was that the video stores were ordering new releases from several distributors at the same time, in an effort to hedge their bets on getting an early airfreight delivery. The video stores and clubs were very competitive. The videos were shipped by airfreight because they wanted to be the first to offer the new titles. They would accept the first shipment, and then refuse any other shipments that arrived later , claiming they were *too* late. To make matters even more intolerable for the distributors, they then had to pay the costly airfreight charges to get their videos back. Then, by the time the videos got back to the distributor's, they were "old news," and the market for them was no longer hot.

The distributors didn't want to run the risk of getting stuck again with a load of stale inventory. Since Paramount Pictures was already committed to their announced release of *Star Trek II, The Wrath of Kahn*, they could see the problem looming ahead. The distributors were ordering in very small quantities to control their losses. This, of course, entirely destroyed the profitability for the movie companies.

I had a solution for them. It was not rocket science, but it would get the distribution under control so the distributors would feel comfortable knowing that no other distributor would get the new titles before them, and that everyone would get a fair shot. There would no longer be any advantage in the video stores ordering a new release from more than one distributor because everyone would get them at the same time. I named it *Time Controlled Release*.

Since I didn't have any money to invest in my venture, I set up an agreement with an airfreight forwarder that they would pay me a commission on all the freight I brought them. As a consultant in a private consulting practice, I would receive twenty percent of all the freight billing. When I sold Paramount Pictures on the concept, the agreement was that they would not pay me, but I would take responsibility for selecting the airfreight forwarders, getting the best prices, and running everything smoothly. I was to be their consultant for free.

> *"Success is not measured by how high you fly, but how high you bounce."*
> Bits and Pieces

The first month I cleared more money than I made in the two years prior. In no time at all, Columbia Pictures called and asked if I would provide the same service for them. . . I would. . . I did. The next month netted one hundred thirty-five thousand dollars! After that the money became even more serious as I kept adding more movie companies to my client list.

I was extremely busy. My wife and I had started the consulting business on our dining room table. With the rapid growth of the video industry, and my expanding client base, I began having problems with the freight forwarder I was using. I had to start my own airfreight company just to keep up the level of service. This, of course, also added to my profits.

All this time I was constantly marketing. I was often asked why was I still marketing when we were so busy. I simply asked, "Why does Coke or Pepsi still advertise?" I never let up on the marketing, yet I always kept my name out of the trade papers that wanted stories about my success. There was no point in educating or motivating my competitors.

The best way to dominate this business was to keep my name in front of the movie companies. Sure, it was expensive, but can you imagine how expensive it would be for the competition to market as much as I was? Of course if they decided to do that, they would have to spend as much money and only get in return that which they could take away from me. In the meantime, I had all the business, and that in itself made the heavy marketing affordable. But all that was after I already had gotten the business with virtually no advertising. Sometimes you have to advertise to keep business, even though you didn't have to advertise to get it.

I moved the operation from our dining room table to a rented warehouse. Less than a year later I moved it again to a sixty thousand square foot warehouse, with forty-seven offices on four and a quarter acres with a railroad siding. I bought this building for nine hundred thousand dollars with no money down because it was a foreclosure, in rough shape, and nobody wanted it. I then borrowed a million dollars with the building as collateral. A year and a half later, when I decided to retire, I sold it for one and a half million dollars.

While attending a video distributor's convention in Washington D.C., I called back to my Chicago office and received a message from a Canadian woman who had extensive airfreight experience and wanted to know if I needed another Canadian agent. I called her, and in six hours over the phone, set up a Canadian company that duplicated my entire operation in the U.S. She became my Canadian vice-president. It cost twenty-three thousand U.S. dollars to set up the company, which I sold to her upon my retirement fourteen months later—for four hundred thousand dollars!

By now I had agents in every commercial airport city across the U.S., and one hundred and forty-seven salaried employees in the U.S. and Canada. The volume of my business had grown to the point where I was carrying as much as two million dollars in accounts receivable with the movie companies. Even though business was good, the accounts receivable were becoming burdensome, and still growing. I had built my quality of service by paying my agents within fifteen days of billing me. I needed to do something because I was trying to pay it out faster than it was coming in. It would be most difficult to approach the major movie companies for faster payment, while at the same time marketing for even more business.

I needed a solution. Should I go back to using self-hypnosis for an idea? Since my car was so good for self-hypnosis in the past, I went back to my favorite parking spot under a big shady tree. I found it much easier now to relax in a big luxury car than it was just a short while ago in a small compact car. I found it even easier to visualize success since I now had already experienced my first month of making a million dollars. In minutes I was back in self-hypnosis.

I don't think I was in hypnosis for more than a few minutes when the idea came to me. This was without a doubt a solution.

I created a new company called Transportation Financial Services (TFS). Its function was to collect accounts receivable and manage accounts payable for freight companies. I hired a full time attorney and transferred all my accounting employees to the new company. I immediately sent letters to all my clients advising them that TFS was now handling all of my accounts receivable, and that in the future they should pay them directly. This new company of mine was as aggressive as a bulldog. If someone didn't pay within thirty days, they got a letter soon followed by a phone call requesting payment. On a few occasions I got complaints about their aggressiveness from the movie companies, and I just said, "I know. . . they're a little aggressive, but they do a good job for me. I'm sorry—I'll speak to them about it."

This accelerated my cash flow nicely. Next, we sent a letter to all our agents explaining that Transportation Financial Services was now handling all my accounts payable, and that all accounts would now be paid within forty-five days rather than the fifteen days they were accustomed to. This slowed down our payouts by another thirty days. None of my agents wanted to lose the very profitable business they were getting from me, so they all accepted the later payment.

I now had my receivables in hand for thirty days before I had to pay them out. Since this was as much as two million dollars, the monthly interest on the float was enough to pay the attorney and the entire accounting staff with several thousand a month left over for me. Lesson learned:

> **The brain is faster than hands for making money.**

What disappointed me was that my accountant was totally amazed at this idea. It appeared to me that he should have thought of it himself since he started with me from the very beginning and should have understood my business completely. Instead, I later realized that my business had far outgrown his expertise and that he was in way over his head. I discovered this when I finally insisted he explain some figures that I couldn't understand. I told him we weren't

24

moving ahead until he could explain things to my complete satisfaction. In my constant hectic flurry of travel between Hollywood and New York, I had been forced to trust his judgment and ability without totally understanding the accounting. Things were going great! What's there to understand? Lesson learned:

You must always know where you're at.

It turned out that my trusted accountant had made an error some months back, and didn't know how to cover it up. I fired him on the spot. He was trying to cover up an error of over a million dollars in overstated profits. To demonstrate his audacity, he even billed me thousands for his last month of work—even though the work was useless.

By this time I had already been through four attorneys. I finally found a reliable and honest one after the fourth or fifth attempt. My experience with attorneys had been nothing but disappointing. They were either too busy, or unreliable. One referred me to an accountant and the two of them together wasted over a hundred thousand dollars. You may wonder how this happened, but keep in mind that I was operating a business that kept me running all the time. These were the professionals I hired to protect me. On our twenty-fifth wedding anniversary my wife gave me a plaque that said: "Love many, trust few, and always paddle your own canoe." Lesson learned:

No one minds your money as well as you.

They say no tree grows up to the sky. By now the video industry was maturing. Home videos were no longer holding a price of eighty-nine dollars and ninety-five cents. In fact, they were even being offered for five dollars with the purchase of a hamburger in some places. The writing was on the wall. Soon the urgency of getting the videos first would be gone, and they would be trucked rather than flown. I already had a fleet of my own trucks in place and a network of trucking companies to complete a nationwide system.

By now I had grown tired of the business and knew what it would take to ward off the competition once the business went to ground transportation. I had been constantly marketing to keep the competition out. It was no longer a secret—this was big business and they wanted in. They were offering rates that they couldn't afford to maintain because it was below their cost of moving the videos. They just wanted to get their feet in the door, and then they would try to make a profit once they got established. I held them off until I was ready to quit. Then I backed off and let them in—by then there was nothing left. Several of them went bankrupt shortly thereafter. They worked for nothing hoping to get a bite of the juicy apple and once they got in found nothing but the core. Lesson learned:

Know when to let go.

I thought I'd retire. I tried it and failed. I say failed because I gave up. I've decided that retirement is an outdated concept—at least for me. I wanted to do several things yet: prove to myself that I could create something successful again, pursue my interest in the mind and hypnotism, and work toward becoming an old master rather than an old geezer. I've achieved some of these goals already. But to become an old master some day, I'll have to help many people realize their goals and dreams. That's what this book is about—your success.

Remember, success is a decision. Let's go develop that decision.

CHAPTER ONE

Do You Get The Picture?

Everything I say may not initially appear to suit your needs, but with   minor twists you may find ways to use most methods in your practice or business.

Do You Get The Picture?

"If you really want to do something you'll find a way; if you don't, you'll find an excuse."

Author Unknown

Most of these principles apply in all businesses. My marketing classes consist of hypnotherapists, psychotherapists, chiropractors, contractors, homebuilders, marketing people, consultants and entrepreneurs.

Set Your Sights High

One of the things you've got to do is set your sights high. You may have been taught to not "pipe dream," but remember the fleas and elephants stories. Not allowing yourself to have dreams is reinforcing the self-limiting beliefs that were instilled by others. Psychotherapists and hypnotists know that success is dependent on reinforcement. It can be self-reinforcement or by others, or better yet, both.

If you set your sights low enough, you'll surely get there. But is that true success? If you set them high and fall a little short of your mark, you'll still be ahead.

Do You Get The Picture?

"The universe is full of magical things patiently waiting for our wits to grow sharper."

Eden Phillpotts (1862—1960)
Writer

Invest some time in researching the total scope of your venture. Be sure you know its full potential. Don't make the mistake of not realizing how big your opportunity is and miss your mark.

A few years ago I flew with my family to Alaska on a combined business and pleasure trip. I had been enchanted by a photograph I had seen years earlier of a car pulled off to the side of the road in Denali Park. The driver was standing alongside his car looking off in the distance at an incredible view of Mt. McKinley, snowcapped and golden in the sunshine. I wanted to drive to Denali Park and see Mt. McKinley. When I inquired at the hotel they laughed, and explained to me that you only get a view of Mt. McKinley from the road like that about twice a year.

Not wanting to accept no for an answer, I called the local airport and arranged to be flown to Mt. McKinley the next day. The older single engine plane was a treat in itself. It had a windshield that curved up overhead into the leading edge of the roof. It was a beautiful August day with bright sunshine as we took off and banked away from the sun. As

29

Do You Get The Picture?

we climbed to ten thousand feet, which was the maximum height in that plane, the weather changed to hazy and gray.

We flew a while and I kept peering ahead expecting to see the peak in the distance at any time soon. By now all I could see was gray and a little blowing snow. Suddenly the pilot said, "Well, there she is." I peered forward and saw nothing but gray. "No not there, there!" He was pointing up through the rooftop part of the windshield. I looked up and there it was. Golden in the sunlight, thirteen thousand feet above us, the peak of Mt. McKinley. I had no idea where to look! I had set my sights far too low. What I was looking at through the front of the windshield was a gray wall—the face of a sheer vertical mountain wall! It's a good thing I wasn't flying the plane. Not knowing how big the picture was, I would have blindly flown into the wall.

"As long as you're going to think anyway—then you might as well think BIG!"

Donald Trump
Business Executive

See who's successful in your field and see what they're doing that you can match now, and what your goal for the future should be to improve on their service or sales. No matter how eager you are to get started, a false start can be costly. So spend a little extra time investigating and planning your goals.

Some People Can't Get The Big Picture

When I had an airfreight sales staff, we had a weekly sales meeting geared to increase sales and improve customer relations. I handled all the movie companies myself, but the sales staff's responsibility was to acquire other business. What I did after the sales meetings seemed more productive than the meetings themselves.

Each week after the meeting, I'd ask a couple of the salespeople to individually stop in my office and see me because I had a couple of leads for them. I'd time each meeting fifteen minutes apart. When they came into my office, I'd ask how they were doing and then give them a slip of paper saying, "I've been told there's a good possibility that these companies ship by air and are not one hundred per cent satisfied with their present freight forwarder." Usually I only gave them three leads because they would work that number of leads thoroughly. I found that they most often would come back with one or two new accounts. As each salesperson left my private office with his new "hot" leads, I'd open my lower desk drawer, take out the phone directory, and copy down three more *hot* leads for the next salesman.

My salesmen all had access to the Chicago yellow pages phone directory, but didn't use it for leads. They believed good leads had to be hard to get, and let that self-limiting belief stop them from dipping into that treasure trove. The phone book was apparently too easy and unsophisticated for them. This is the same as me looking out the window of the airplane with my sights set too low. The opportunity was so large for airfreight sales that the salesmen couldn't see the whole picture. In fact, when I was selling airfreight, on most days I only worked until noon. That's all it took to do more than the average "good" salesman, and much more in sales than my employer expected. The simple fact was: most salesmen didn't really work hard.

Those That Got The Picture

In the movie *Cocktail,* Tom Cruise plays a bartender that took the ordinary task of tending bar a step further than most bartenders and turned it into an art form. There was a strong message in this movie that's plot was so weak I've long forgotten it. The message was that you could take something a step beyond what everyone else does and make a big success of it.

I was in the habit of picking up a morning paper and coffee at the local 7-Eleven for some time, when one morning there was a new face at the counter. This woman was so pleasant and friendly that it was a true contrast to what I was accustomed to from any 7-Eleven counter. She treated me as though I was spending hundreds of dollars even though it was really less than two. I remarked that she was a new face in the store, and she pleasantly explained that this was her first job in many years. She had been a stay at home mom, and now her kids were all in school full time. She obviously was putting her heart into her job. For two weeks I enjoyed starting my morning off with her efficiency, pleasant smile and attitude. Then one morning she was gone.

I asked the owner what happened to the new girl. "She doesn't work here any more," was his curt answer. I didn't push it, even though I was curious as to what happened to her.

Do You Get The Picture?

A few weeks later I stopped in the same store, but on the way home this time. There she was. Only this time she was very well dressed and in high heels on the customer side of the counter. "I missed you the last two weeks," I said. "Oh, Hi! I don't work here anymore. A nice man that used to come in here every morning hired me to work in his company. I've got a wonderful job with great benefits and for lots more money. I'm an administrative assistant."

She got the picture.

"It is the greatest of all mistakes to do nothing because you can only do a little. Do what you can."
Sydney Smith (1771—1845)
Clergyman and Writer

She saw work as an opportunity—an opportunity to flex her abilities and to see what she could become. I suspect that by now she's management.

Others That Got The Picture

In the past, we were accustomed to businesses being small in scale. Sure there were the Sears stores, the Woolworth's and Kresge's, but for the most part, hardware stores, toy stores, stationery stores, and the like were small operations. Then, what evolved is what we came to call the "Category Killers."

Do You Get The Picture?

They all saw the bigger picture and took the marketing one step further. Here are just a few examples of marketing being taken a step further:

1. Home Depot = Hardware Stores

2. Toys R Us = Toy Stores/Department Stores

3. Kinko's = Copies/Currency Exchanges

4. Office Depot = Stationery Stores

5. Kinder Care = Baby Sitting/Child Care

6. Frames R Us = Picture Frames

7. Wal-Mart = General Merchandise

8. Radio Shack = Home Electronics

9. Petsmart = Pet Stores

These are all companies that developed by taking their respective businesses one step further than anyone before them. They saw the big picture, the "Top of the mountain." That's why it's important for you to fully understand the scope of your opportunity, so you start off with your sights focused and properly geared for all that your opportunity entails. A little extra time doing this is time invested—not time wasted.

Your Commitment to Your Success

> *"Obsession doesn't guarantee success. On the other hand, a lack of it does guarantee failure."*
>
> *Tom Peters*
> *Business Writer and Speaker*

As I said earlier, and it's worth repeating many times, success is a decision not good fortune. **If you're determined to succeed, you will.**

If you've surveyed your opportunity well, you have an idea what kind of commitment your success will entail. Your commitment is the key factor here. Many, many people have absolutely no idea what the word commitment really means. Today, everyone from some of our presidents to the cleaning lady has a very loose understanding of the word commitment. Those whose understanding is equally loose, will probably allow the cart of effort to roll back down over them just as they've pushed it three-fourths of the way to the top of the hill of success.

The difference between "doing" a business, and being "in" a business is your commitment. You must be **committed**. If you are truly committed, you will without question be **in** the business—doing it will come automatically.

Do You Get The Picture?

Think about this: In a bacon and egg breakfast, the chicken is **involved**—the pig is **committed**.

I've always thought it is easy to succeed since all you have to do is see what others are doing, and then do it better and do more. **That's really all there is to it!** Where the commitment comes in, is to what length do you have to go to—to do more and do it better? And, are you willing to do it? This is an excellent time to remind you of the importance of knowing all that's entailed in your venture—seeing the whole picture. Having thoroughly done that, you're equipped to make an informed decision.

"Success, real success, in any endeavor demands more from an individual than most people are willing to offer—not more than they are capable of offering."
                                                              James Roche

Some years ago I began publishing a newsletter. I thought I had a pretty good understanding of all that it entailed. It was successful, but not to my satisfaction. I had over a hundred thousand dollars in subscription sales when I realized how long publishers operate at a loss before they realize any profit. Since this was only a newsletter, it wasn't going to take as long as most, but longer than I wanted for the amount of work involved. The commitment required was greater than I was prepared to make. I would have saved a lot of time and energy if I had only slowed down enough to get a better view of the total picture.

How Much is Enough?

"Money doesn't make you happy,
but it quiets the nerves."
Sean O'Casey (1880—1964)
Playwright

I've been told by some people that I'm too success oriented, and that they're, *"ahem . . .* more into spiritual things." That's always been a pet peeve of mine. If they're so spiritual, why don't they apply themselves and give the excess money to the deserving needy? I've found many deserving causes. It's not difficult at all to find them. How spiritual are you if you're gifted with ability and don't use it for the benefit of others? I've met many lazy people using their spirituality as an excuse.

Do You Get The Picture?

*"The man who rolls up his shirt
sleeves is rarely in danger of losing
his shirt."*

                                   Bits and Pieces

For many who shy away from doing what's necessary to
succeed, it is simply fear. Not fear of success—plain
ordinary fear. Somewhere someone came up with the idea to
say that, "they just start to become successful and then
sabotage themselves." That claim presupposes success. As if
they can readily achieve it. "Oh, I'm above struggling to
succeed, I just sabotage myself when I'm approaching it."
That satisfies their ego by downplaying *your* ability to
succeed. It's as if to say they can easily do what you're
trying to do, or have done. They just have this one little quirk
that they sabotage themselves because they're afraid of
success. Don't buy that! You're doing it, they aren't, can't,
or won't—period. If there is such a thing as fear of success,
learn to discipline yourself to overcome your fear. Then
when someone tells you how successful they could have
been, you can say, "Oh yes, I had that fear too. But I've
worked my way through it and overcame it."

CHAPTER TWO

Become a "Joiner"

"Being bored is an insult to oneself."
    Jules Renard (1864—1910)
                Writer

Become actively involved in appropriate groups. There's most likely an abundance of groups related to what you're doing, or organizations that would normally contain a number of people that could become your clients or customers. Don't be an obvious opportunist by running around at your first few functions handing out your business cards. Most organizations recognize those tactics as an indication of a person only out for what they can get.

"The shortest way to do many things is to do one thing at a time."
Samuel Smiles (1812—1904)
Physician and Writer

You'll need to get genuinely involved. That means getting to know everyone and then volunteering to help out with functions. There's no easy shortcut to this, so be sure you can devote the time necessary. It's smart to join and become involved in as many groups as you realistically can, but be sure to not overextend yourself. Once the recognition starts, you'll find that they'll depend on you for assistance. This is great because when they, or someone they know, needs your professional services, it becomes almost automatic that the business is yours. I found business after hours groups and an abundance of business/social groups that provide opportunities like this. If you have no idea where to look for these groups, check with your local Chamber of Commerce. You may as well get to know them. They'll come in handy in other instances that we'll cover later.

Become A Joiner

*"Five words that stand between you
and your dream:
I DON'T FEEL LIKE IT."*
                                    Bits and Pieces

I became involved in several groups. In some instances the
only initial benefit was that because I volunteered for so
many projects, I always knew what was going on. People
started calling me with their questions. Soon that spilled over
into them viewing me as a person of authority—not a bad
place to be when you need to create a professional image.

Success and Wealth Through Focused Concentration

*"I was seldom able to see an
opportunity until it ceased to be one."*
                                    *Mark Twain (1835—1910)
                                    Writer and Humorist*

Become A Joiner

Use Focused Concentration for your business planning and creativity, which is right brain work and should be done in the alpha state. (The alpha state is a state of deep relaxation that creates a bridge between the conscious and subconscious minds.) The alpha brain wave range is an area where visualization and creativity can be stimulated. Execution of your plans is left brain work and should be done in the beta state. (The beta state is a state of mental alertness). In school we are taught to think with our left brain, but our creativity comes from our right brain. As Einstein said, "Imagination is more important than intelligence." You have to learn how to use our right brain for creating and planning in your business. You should then use your left brain for executing your plans.

Learning to daydream is important to your success. Practice Focused Concentration and you will become good at it. Focus on assuming the role of your prospective clients'. Always ask yourself: "How can I better serve my clients' needs?" Try to experience those needs. Whenever I develop any marketing plan, I first look at my client's needs through their eyes while in Focused Concentration, and write my advertising addressing those needs.

"It may be that those who do most, dream most."
Stephen Leacock (1869—1944)
Economist and Humorist

42

Become A Joiner

Earlier I mentioned self-hypnosis. You don't need to be a master of self-hypnosis to focus your concentration on a specific question or challenge. Focused Concentration is what you attempt to achieve when you close a door to shut out the kids' noise and the TV in the other room when you're trying to work on your taxes or balance your checkbook. Most of our thinking is done in the midst of noise and other activities, and often we have to think and make decisions while doing other work or chores.

Many people find that a drive on the open road is a good time for them to think. That's because distractions are at a minimum. For most people it's not too often that they can take time away from everyone and everything to just think. This is exactly what you should do to access the parts of your brain that will assure your success. I know it's hard to take the time, and at first you may not even appreciate its true value. But once you start doing this, you'll find out how well it works and you'll make it an important part of your method of operation.

Getting Started

"The future starts today, not tomorrow."

Pope John Paul II

43

Become A Joiner

At a time when you can set aside a quiet half hour, find a place where you will not be interrupted by the phone or by anyone. If you have a family pet around, you may want to exclude it from the room so it doesn't spoil your concentration by wanting attention. Find a comfortable chair to relax in. Put your feet up, or flat on the floor. Do not have your ankles crossed, as later they will break your concentration by cutting off your circulation. (If you're going to do this in the evening when you're tired, you may want to sit up in a less than totally relaxing chair lest you fall asleep.) Adjust yourself so you're able to relax—loosen any tight clothing, take your shoes off, etc.

We are all "hard wired" the same in that the simple procedure I'm going to describe to you works for everyone. If not extremely well at first, it certainly will after a little practice. **Anyone** can do this well.

"Before I can sell John Doe what John Doe buys, I must see the world through John Doe's eyes."
Bits and Pieces

State your intended purpose for the session just before starting, i.e. "What benefits are my prospects looking for?" This will eliminate the need for a lot of conscious thought when you're ready to open up your creativity.

Note: *In this exercise you'll be rolling your eyes up. If you wear contacts, either remove them or compensate for them.*

Become A Joiner

This simple procedure is most easily learned in three steps. First, roll up your eyes into your forehead as though you were looking through your forehead at your hairline (or where your hairline should be if you have none). Second, **keeping your eyes rolled up into your forehead,** slowly close your eyelids while taking in a deep breath and holding it. Third, relax your eyes, exhale, and relax your body allowing yourself to float down into deep relaxation.

While relaxing, imagine seeing the doors of a custom elevator. This will be your custom elevator, so the doors can be made of whatever material you like. The doors can be of stainless steel, or brass, or bronze, or anything you prefer— even gold. Since the price is right, why not?

Then, imagine your elevator doors slowly opening as you look inside. The interior of your elevator can be however you like. It can be large or small. It can be luxurious or ordinary. The walls can be of whatever material you like. They can be richly paneled, covered with fine fabric, stainless steel walls, or even glass. The floor can be tiled with rich marble, plushly carpeted, or simply covered with ordinary tile or carpet. As you step into your elevator, allow the doors to close, and notice the numbers indicating that you're at the twenty-fifth floor.

As you continue relaxing, visualize the numbers slowly descending. With each passing number, begin to focus your attention on relaxing all your body parts, starting with your scalp. As you visualize each descending number and focus on relaxing each body part, you will find your relaxation becoming deeper and deeper. By the time you get down to the first floor, you should have yourself relaxed sufficiently to access your right brain in ways that you're probably not regularly accustomed to. I like to open my elevator doors and step out into a favorite place, where I relax on a comfortable bench to contemplate whatever my purpose is for being there.

Now is the time to think about the question or issue you selected earlier when you stated your intention. Allow yourself to continue relaxing as you calmly review your subject matter, allowing your mind to just wander around and through the issue or question. Don't concern yourself with whether or not the thoughts are practical—that's left brain interference. Tell your left brain that you'll consult with it later, before moving ahead with anything.

You may come up with immediate answers, and you may not. If nothing obvious immediately develops, don't be disappointed. That's how it works a good part of the time. (That's how it was for me with my multi-million dollar idea.) Be pleased and satisfied with your efforts. Your subconscious mind has now been alerted to your intention and can work on it later, as you go on about your activities and even while you sleep.

Have you ever bought a car and then noticed that there were a lot more of the same car of the same color around than you had previously realized? That's because your subconscious is now aware that that's the car you like. Now it will bring your conscious attention to every one that it sees. Your subconscious has been seeing them all along—it just didn't know you were interested.

Every time you practice Focused Concentration, you're notifying your subconscious mind of your interests and putting it's power to work for you.

You can add a very effective variation to this practice when you're using it for creative work, by keeping a tablet next to you. Do the exercise with a pen or pencil in your hand.

Become A Joiner

When you've reached your first floor, or favorite place, state your intention to write notes as ideas come to you, and that after writing each note, you will again relax and go into Focused Concentration. Start reviewing the issues and as each idea comes to you, open your eyes and make a very brief note (only one or two words to jog your memory later). Then immediately close your eyes, relax deeply again, and proceed with your thoughts. Each time a new thought pops into your mind, repeat the procedure.

When you're finished, you will be amazed with your ability. You had it in you all the time. Now you're using more of your brain—and in a more effective way.

This system has never failed me.

If you experience difficulty with falling asleep while practicing Focused Concentration, you can change any of three things. Change the time of day, change your chair or recliner, or count down from the fifteenth floor instead of the twenty-fifth. Students often tell me that their mind tends to drift and that they mentally wander around back and forth from their intended issue. If you experience that, you're doing fine. Your right brain functions this way when you're that deeply relaxed. What you'll develop when your mind is right on focus, pays enough dividends to put you far ahead of where you would have been with ordinary concentration. It appears that when the focus is so intense, your mind will "float off course" from time to time—almost like wandering off to the edge of sleep. As long as part of the time your mind is productive, you can consider this a sign that you're doing it right.

Become A Joiner

*"The "haves" and the "have nots"
can be traced back to the "dids" and
the "did nots."*

Anthony Kloc

CHAPTER THREE

Compelling Sales Concept

Developing your Compelling Sales Concept (CSC) is an important task that provides you with an excellent opportunity to use your new Focused Concentration skills. I can't express enough, the importance of creating an **excellent** Compelling Sales Concept. Notice I didn't say a **good** concept? It's well worth your time to devote a lot of consideration to the creation of your CSC because it will appear in all your marketing efforts and on everything you have printed (if you're using it right).

Compelling Sales Concept

This will be your identity or the concept that you want to become known for. It should be unique and attention getting in a way that sets you apart from others.

Take just a moment and think of any CSCs currently advertised. I've listed a few just to give you the idea so you can start thinking about yours.

- Empire Carpet (Call Empire today, carpet tomorrow.)

- Domino's Pizza (Pizza in a half hour.)

- Jewel Foods (Buy one get one free.)

- Craftsman Tools (No questions asked replacement guarantee.)

- Rolls Royce (High price unbelievable quality.)

- 1-800-Flowers (Instant flowers by phone.)

- Seattle FilmWorks (Free film.)

- Godiva Chocolates (High price, status.)

- B.M.W. (Expensive price—status.)

"You either have to be first, best, or different."
Loretta Lynn
Country Music Singer

Compelling Sales Concept

A way to be successful is to amaze people. Keep this in mind as it may take you a while to come up with something. The more people are amazed, the more likely they are to talk about your services or product, and the more likely they are to remember you. If you find yourself stumped in the following exercise, don't be concerned. Selecting a CSC can be a very lengthy process. You can always implement a good idea later (after testing). I once spent two weeks working with a man that has a doctorate in theology putting together a four-word statement. We kept going back and forth with it until it was exactly correct.

If you're eager to get started and tempted to not spend time completing the following worksheet, you're fooling yourself into not starting out on a solid foundation. Even if you don't complete it to your satisfaction at your first attempt, let your subconscious mind learn what you're trying to accomplish and it may just pop into your head while you're doing other things.

I found out that my attorney, who I always thought was a genius at writing letters, spends as much as two days writing a short letter. By the time he's done, the letter perfectly describes exactly what he means. If an attorney and a doctor put this kind of effort into saying exactly what they mean, don't you think you can allow yourself a little time to come up with an excellent CSC? Name your CSC as carefully as you would name your first child. Your CSC should appear everywhere—all marketing of any kind should include your CSC.

<u>CSC—Worksheet</u>

1. List the three best reasons why your clients do business with you over a competitor or use an alternative to your methods or products.

1)_____

_____

_____

_____

_____

_____

2)_____

_____

_____

_____

_____

3)_____

_____

_____

_____

_____

_____

2. Who is your market? Who exactly should your target be?

_____

_____

_____

_____

_____

_____

_____

3. What are the three primary benefits your customer expects from the purchase of your product or service?

1)_____

_____

_____

_____

_____

2) _____

_____

_____

_____

_____

_____

3) _____

_____

_____

_____

_____

4. Describe your specific market and their main problem by completing this sentence:

   Do you know how . . .

   _____

   _____

   _____

   _____

   _____

   _____

Compelling Sales Concept

5. Describe how you solve that problem by completing this sentence:

Well, what I do is . . .

_____

_____

_____

_____

_____

_____

_____

6. Now utilize the information from #4 and #5 into a direct statement that represents your *compelling concept.*

_____

_____

_____

_____

_____

_____

7. Now, if possible, condense the statement in #6 to a suitable business slogan brief enough for business cards or stationery.

_____

_____

_____

_____

_____

_____

Friends and family make poor tests or critics for your work.

After you've created your CSC, you may want to ask the opinion of your family and friends. If you do, don't let them sway your decision either way on a CSC. Some will like everything you do, yet others may not be encouraging on anything you create. You'll need to get other opinions before making a decision, and don't forget—no decision has to be final. It's best though, to sit on your CSC for a bit, just to make sure it satisfies you and your needs. Once you start printing it everywhere, it'll be costly to change.

Like Jumping Out of a Plane

I'll give you a long list of suggestions you can use. Taking them is up to you. It's much like the suggestion that when jumping out of a plane—take a parachute with you.

Compelling Sales Concept

Building a practice or a business is not easy. If it was, everyone would be doing it—then it would then become difficult because there would be far too much competition. So we have to face it. We have to do everything better than the other guy. Once you accept that fact, it gets simple. Just do it!

Notice? I said simple—not easy.

The fact that you're reading this book is an indication that you're willing to do more than the average person. The average person doesn't read, let alone read a book on marketing. Once you implement the things you're getting here, you have to think like a farmer. A farmer has to have the faith that while it's October and he's plowing his fields for a future crop, that there will certainly be one if he follows through with all the other necessary steps.

I had a graduate student that decided to only apply a few of the techniques given here. She picked and chose a few that she applied for a few days, and then abandoned them. She didn't have the faith that they would work. Next she hired someone to consult with her at one hundred forty dollars an hour for a minimum of a week. That didn't work either. The reason? She didn't apply herself in either case. She's now back at her full time job where she belongs. Where someone will again tell her all day, every day, exactly what she is to do. She understands that. Everyone is not cut out for building and maintaining a practice or business.

CHAPTER FOUR

Risk Elimination

Risk Elimination is as important as having a CSC before planning your advertising. You need your CSC and your Risk Elimination planned so you have something to advertise. The combination of the two should appear in all your ads. Remember, just advertising by announcing your business or practice won't bring enough business to make you successful.

Clients and customers are not always willing to take the risk involved with something not meeting their expectations. If you assume that risk, you eliminate a major obstacle to their decision. Don't be afraid to offer some sort of valuable Risk Elimination. Research has proven over and over again that Risk Elimination pays, and pays big!

"Plunge boldly into the   thick of life."

Goethe (1749—1832)

Writer

Even though Risk Elimination increases revenue, many professionals don't practice it. The reason? Fear! They're afraid that they'll lose money. My feeling is that if you lose money with a Risk Elimination program, you'd better look at the quality of your service or product. If people are getting what they were promised, there's no reason Risk Elimination won't work. In any event, after you've tried it, if it doesn't work for you, you can always discontinue offering and promoting it.

Once you've tried it and found how well it works, promote it heavily.

When I held the grand opening for my carwash I offered a free wash without any purchase (the ultimate of Risk Elimination—no risk.) People lined up in cars for over a block waiting for their free wash. After their free wash, so many people pulled up to the gas pumps to show their appreciation, that it actually paid to do it. Most people appreciate a good deal and want to do the right thing.

Risk Elimination

Another feature of offering the free carwash was that I amazed people.

Depending on your practice or business, you will have to make the necessary adjustments to make it workable for you. Here's an opportunity for a little right-brained creativity.

There are several approaches that can be taken:

♦ Offer a total refund with a reasonable time limit.

♦ Offer more than a total refund with a premium of some sort (keep the free booklet, gadget, or something of value, etc.).

♦ Provide emotional risk reduction. This is good where a refund is impractical as in many private practices. You can offer a free evaluation session, free exam, or free initial consultation. For many practices, this is time you might be spending on their first visit anyway. With this already behind you, you can immediately proceed with your services, or at least save time when they come back for their first appointment.

Don't show disappointment if they don't decide to proceed with you at that time. They may come back later. If not, they at least now know you, had a positive experience, and you now have their address and phone number to add to your mailing list. They may prove very worthwhile to you later. And as long as you spent time with them, having them leave with a good feeling about

61

you doesn't cost you anything. One thing is certain—if you display any disappointment in their decision, they won't come back.

Marketing of this book is an example of Risk Elimination. I'm promising anyone that buys this book a full refund if they're not satisfied that it will make them money far beyond its cost. In writing this book I am providing so many valuable, proven strategies, that if a person studies and uses it, not only will he not want to return it, he'll tell friends about it. Once a reader recognizes its worth as a reference to go back to frequently, he won't lend it to a friend either. He'll recommend they buy their own.

The following form will assist you in formulating your Risk Elimination program. I suggest that you read the worksheet carefully, and then use Focused Concentration for ideas.

Risk Elimination Worksheet

1. What does your client expect most when purchasing your services?

   _____

   _____

   _____

   _____

Risk Elimination

_____

_____

_____

2. Based on what result your customer is seeking, write down exactly what "satisfaction" should be for them. (Be sure to specify a time frame: immediately, 30 days, 12 months, etc.)

_____

_____

_____

_____

_____

_____

_____

_____

3. Describe the most motivating approach you could take to guarantee that result to your clients. (Complete refund of service or purchase price, no-risk trial prior to purchase, etc.)

_____

_____

_____

_____

_____

_____

_____

_____

4.   What free bonus products or services, beyond a refund, could you offer to make your guarantee *better than risk free*?

_____

_____

_____

_____

_____

_____

5.   If your business doesn't lend itself to money-back guarantees (such as real estate, medical practice, legal practice, etc.), what ways could you reduce risk for your clients, customers, or patients? (Consider partial guarantees, informed decision-making aids, free initial consultations, etc.)

_____

_____

_____

Risk Elimination

_____

_____

_____

_____

6. Write out your Risk Elimination offer the way you would
    promote it to your customers.

_____

_____

_____

_____

_____

_____

7. Write down the best strategy for testing your new Risk
    Elimination offer over the next 30 days.

_____

_____

_____

_____

_____

_____

Risk Elimination

Depending on many variables, you may never have to give a refund, or lose a dime on Risk Elimination. However, if you're in a business that exposes you to some losses, it's best to give some time to developing a plan for them. Risk Elimination losses can be turned into additional revenue if you've planned for them by offering alternatives such as a credit for what was already spent, and offering an alternative plan.

If a customer or client didn't get what they came for initially, they still need it. Many business people would mistakenly just accept the refund as a cost of doing business. Why not provide for it in advance, so you don't lose a sale and a client or customer?

A therapist can offer a client a plan supported by an alternative plan during their first encounter. Depending upon the way this is presented to a client, they can be given an understanding that will allow for additional sessions or therapy. This can readily be done by explaining that after a certain term of sessions an evaluation will be made: a determination as to whether or not the progress is satisfactory, and if more sessions are advisable. Later, I'll get into detail about setting up appointments; how many, and how to eliminate no-shows.

You should heavily promote your Risk Elimination plan. It's a big plus to consumers as it eliminates their fear of loss.

Fear of Loss

Fear of loss is one of the most powerful tools you can use. It not only strikes the emotions, it emotes a basic instinct. You should create fear of loss in your advertising at every opportunity. Whenever you successfully create it, you will stimulate your business. Watch people in buffet lines. The way some people pile food on their plates is an architectural accomplishment. They really have no need to because they can go back as often as they like. But fear of loss takes over and they overfill their plates. Only those with good self-control take moderate amounts. I've seen hordes of people on the Oprah Winfrey TV show clamor for a left shoe, with no promise of getting its mate, when she offered a limited number of free samples.

Try offering something to someone with another person present. See if they don't immediately want to know if the offer can be extended to them too. Fear of loss is so strong that even people that know and use it well are still susceptible to it.

To create fear of loss you can offer something for a limited time, or in a limited number. When I do workshops, I usually have enough audiocassettes for everyone that wants to buy one. However, when I announce that they're available, if I only have a few out at one time, people grab them up right away. When they see a pile of them, they think there's no need to hurry. Later, after the enthusiasm has passed, they may decide to just forget it altogether.

Recently, at a convention, I had a bit of a "feeding frenzy" break out for the new light and sound instruments I had just began marketing to hypnotherapists. People were standing three and four deep at times and feeling very fortunate that

Risk Elimination

they got to buy a system. While all this was happening, I was busily observing and making mental notes as to just how it occurred so I could recreate it at will. For months later, people were still calling from across the country to buy systems.

The most important elements were: people were curious but only a few at a time could try a system; the others could only watch and wait their turn. The display itself was intriguing and there were only a few systems in view that could be purchased—even though we had a huge supply. This combination created a fear of loss. In the evening after the exhibits were closed, people were stopping me in the halls wanting information because they were afraid they wouldn't be able to get to talk to me the next day at the exhibit.

The very successful hypnotherapist I interviewed in Ireland, traveled from town to town doing hypnotherapy in hotels that he booked far in advance. He created fear of loss in his pre-arrival ads by limiting the number of clients he could see while in town. When meeting for their current session, people booked for his next tour in advance fearing they might miss out.

CHAPTER FIVE

Advertising

Most advertising principles apply whether in ads, letters, brochures, TV, or radio. The general ideas need to be adjusted to fit the particular situation. Wherever possible, I have made as many of the adjustments necessary for the various advertising media.

Institutional Advertising

The first thing we want to do is discuss the difference between institutional advertising and direct response advertising. Institutional advertising is only practical to major corporations except in a very limited number of

Advertising

situations. Major brand name products are advertised institutionally in that they only advertise the product. They leave it up to you to find where you can get it because it's readily available in a multitude of locations.

This type of advertising for a small business or a private practice is a total waste of money; yet I see new entrepreneurs wasting dollars this way all the time. Many fall victim to a type of institutional ad that I call "ego ads." Sharp telemarketers call owners of a new business or practice and offer them an opportunity to participate in a "special" public service announcement, for an amount that sounds only a little pricey. The truth of the matter is: the fee is outrageous for what the same airtime on that same station could be bought for if you called directly yourself. Most of the price is commission.

The telemarketers know that a new entrepreneur would like nothing better than to hear his name on the air. In fact, most likely the prospect of this appeals to his ego—as though he's nearly arrived since his name is on the air. Ego can tempt very smart people to do very dumb things.

As for the announcement's effectiveness, there's none—period. You might turn on your radio to hear it each time, but that's it. Oh, if you tell your Mom she might listen and tell you it's very nice, but believe me, that's your total true listening audience. I'll cover radio advertising in the next section and explain how you can use it.

Running ads with your name or the name of your practice or business across the top is almost as much a waste of money. Many people believe this is exactly what you should do. This is exactly what you should not do! This is just another variation of an institutional type of ad that only brings minimal results—not nearly enough results for your money.

Advertising

When we look at direct response advertising, you'll see why so many professionals believe it takes so long to build a practice—they're advertising incorrectly!

Direct Response Advertising

How are direct response ads different?

Direct response ads are a call to action. They contain critical elements that compel the reader to call or respond. This is the only type of advertising that represents any real value for small businesses and private practices. You'll see many institutional ads by your colleagues, but just because so many do it, doesn't mean they're getting good value from their advertising dollars. They just don't know any better.

This is where you really want to be able to view the needs of your prospective clients or customers through their eyes. If you can do that accurately, you can write very effective advertising copy. If you're using Focused Concentration, you will be able to do an excellent job of addressing the needs of the readers or listeners.

"You can get everything in life you want, if you will just help enough other people get what they want."
Zig Ziglar
Motivational Speaker

Advertising

The first thing any reader wants to know from your ad is **"What's in it for me?"** If you answer that in the very start of your ad it will pull. Nothing else is more important than that in the beginning of your ad—nothing! Your nameplate is not an important eye-catcher—unless you're already famous and very well known. If your ad is compelling, they'll look for your name and phone. Of course, don't make it difficult to find.

Here's an advertising story. I don't know its origin but it's worth repeating. Two top advertising executives were debating who could write the stronger headline. The first executive, let's call him John Smith, who was the employer of Bob the second executive, bet one hundred dollars there was nothing Bob could write that would compel him to want to read it. Bob took the bet and won. What did he write? "All you wanted to know about John Smith." The point is, people are interested in themselves and whatever benefit you're offering them.

Carefully Consider the Benefits You Offer

"You can't just sell products. You have to sell benefits and solutions."
Bits and Pieces

Lower price itself is not a benefit. When you think about the basic benefit of a lower price, you'll find that the real benefit is it gives one the freedom to spend more money elsewhere. This is the way you have to look into a benefit. What you're looking for is the true primary benefit.

People don't buy quarter inch drills; they buy the ability to drill quarter inch holes. They buy the ability to drill holes where they want them. Can we find other examples of this? What are they buying from you? Analyze this on an individual benefit basis. What do your clients really want from you? If there are many benefits you can offer, you'll need to determine which ones have the most appeal and bring the greatest response.

What is the primary benefit you want to promote? Is it really the benefit? Could you be missing the mark? Would seeing it through your prospect's eyes in Focused Concentration clarify what the benefit should be—or how it should be described?

The first impression a prospect has of you may begin with your ad. While you want to strongly appeal to their need, you want to be sure that it's tasteful and appropriately stated. This is your first opportunity to establish a positive impression of yourself and your business. And this could play a major part in whether or not they decide to do business with you.

Writing Successful Ads

Advertising

*"It takes as much energy to wish as it
does to plan."*
     Eleanor Roosevelt (1884—1962)
     U.S. First Lady and Humanitarian

A good compelling ad will have a clear explanation of the benefits. As I said earlier, I don't sit down to write mediocre ads and good ads. Some ads just turn out to pull better than others. The best approach to this is to be determined to only write good ads.

Plan to devote sufficient lead time so that you can review your ad over a few days, at least. You'll be surprised how differently you'll feel about something you wrote the day before. The chances are you'll find ways to groom and improve your ad several times. For this reason, it's good to save your old notes and rejected copy until you're completely finished. Often parts of discarded ideas will combine well with new ideas and a good ad will come together.

In the sixties I found I could make very nice money buying properties that needed work by fixing and reselling them. The big problem was not getting them in shape; the problem was in finding them. I ran a newspaper ad under the "wanted to buy" classification in the local papers. I got a few calls over several weeks, but not really enough to make it worthwhile. The ad read: "Handyman wants to buy property that needs work." Besides the fact that the number

Advertising

of calls were disappointing, the properties that I was offered were so bad that it would be nearly impossible to make money with them.

I still believed the ad was good because I was getting some calls. Not wanting to call it a bad idea too hastily, I altered the ad just a little. I added the two words: "financially responsible." The ad now read: "Financially responsible handyman wants to buy property that needs work." To this day I don't know exactly what constitutes a financially responsible handyman, but property owners sure wanted to talk to one.

The calls increased, but more importantly, the properties were good. Some needed so little work that I didn't even buy them. I listed them for sale for the people as their real estate broker, and got them good "as-is" prices for their properties.

I wish I could tell you that I determined that people were concerned that handymen could only buy cheap properties. And furthermore, that I determined that they needed a sense of relief from the burden of their property. But the truth is: I wasn't aware. I only sensed that the ad might be good but needed "something." Later I found out that I had unknowingly determined the true benefit that my readers were looking for—relief.

Essentials in Explaining the Benefits in an Ad

Always lead with a compelling headline. The following is a list of words that research has proven to be the most effective and attention getting. Why not use them wherever possible and take the guesswork out of headline writing.

Some Of The Hottest Words in Advertising:

Overrated   High Yield   Formula   Pioneering
Starter Kit   Affordable   Survival   Simplistic
Monitor   Epidemic   Promising Tepid   Sure-Fire
Destiny   Compromise   Technology   Top-Notch
Forecast   Free   Generic   Contrary   Value Line
Obsession   Top Dog   Upscale   Successful
Concept   A Sampler   Measure Up   Unlock   Boom
Bravo!   Heritage   Rewards   Hybrid   Daring
Report Card   Revolution   Monumental   Challenging
Investigative   Scorecard   Envision   Bottom Line
Preppy   Crucial   Round Table   Luxury
Avoiding   Insatiable   Recruiting   Merit   Philosophy
Imagination   Energy   Show Me   Exercising Soar
Liberated   Big Wheel   Panache   Dividends   Test
Drive   Portfolio   Perspective   Foothold   Sensitive
Alert   Lifeblood   Innovative   Dynamics
Spotlight   Masterpiece   Take Action   Distinguished
Under priced   Shrewd   Energize   Novel   Deliver
Last-Minute   Reminiscent   Specialized   Hex

Advertising

Deserve   Cost Shifting   Lavish   Bonanza   Growth
Last Chance   Enterprising   Lively New   Longevity
Best-Selling   Exploit   Excitement   Spiral   Below
Cost   Discovery   Revealing   Effective   Savvy
Skill   Reviewing   Surging   Nest-Egg   Nostalgic
Allure   Mainstream   Ultimate   Launching
Gut Feelings   Revisited   Top-Rated   Just In Time
High Tech   Fueling   Eye-Opening   Breakthrough
Blockbusting   Economic Needs   Fundamentals
Lively Market   Comprehensive   Competitive Edge

Advertising

Always make a specific compelling offer. I have found that you can give people a long list of any items or services that should immediately gain their interest, yet they don't seem to recognize the value of all the items. However, I have taken only one item off the list and promoted it very strongly and enthusiastically, and people would look it over carefully and with interest.

I learned this lesson well when I found myself doing just that many years ago on a property that I bought. As a real estate agent I had access to a multitude of listings. In fact, I had too many. I was looking for a house to buy for myself, preferably one with income. I was watching for something to come up that would represent a good investment for me and not having much luck.

One day while sitting around the office discussing the various listings with each other, one of the agents mentioned that he thought we should be able to sell one house in particular because he thought it was a good buy. I knew that particular listing but had passed it up. After our discussion though, I took another look at the listing, and then another look at the house. It was a good buy. I had missed it!

I bought the house and later sold it at a very nice profit. I often thought back to that scenario and learned from it. Why didn't I see the value myself the first time I saw the house? The answer is simple: I needed someone to focus my attention on it; there were so many listings that my attention was scattered among them. It was as if there were too many choices for me. Not until someone focused my attention to one particular listing, could I see the value in it.

The same need for focus was true with a travel club that I developed. I could advertise a list of outstanding travel bargains with only a mediocre response. But if I isolated one

Advertising

trip, or one cruise, and enthusiastically promoted it alone, everyone appreciated its value and the response was strong. Yet that same cruise was lost in a list of bargains.

This need to be focused seems to be human nature. I learned from this home buying experience and found the knowledge useful in marketing strategy as well as dealing with people. Remember the airfreight salesmen story? They needed their attention focused on a few prospects—not a phone book full.

This factor of human nature is so valuable that I use it whenever I develop advertising, whether it's a mailing piece, sales letter, a radio or TV spot, or a magazine ad. Since I always have so much going on, it's a temptation to want to advertise more than one event or item at a time to save advertising dollars. I don't do it. I've learned that I can generate interest if I enthusiastically promote one item or event, but if I promote more, the response drops. The only way I found around this is if I feature one event or item and have it totally dominate the ad, and then list the secondary item in a smaller way lower in the ad.

I'm even applying this concept in the light and sound mind machines I'm marketing. I have machines that can be used for a multitude of purposes. When someone comes to a therapist, or hypnotherapist, they come for a specific problem or with a specific request. The hypnotherapist can offer them a mind machine that can be used for everything, but he can also offer them a machine for a specific purpose. A person that comes in for sports enhancement hypnosis, does not want a "catch-all" system. He wants a sports enhancement light and sound system. A person that comes in for self-hypnosis wants a self-hypnosis system. The same is true with weight loss: they want a weight loss system—not a system that does everything. I've also produced light and sound machines for learning, sleep, and even golf.

People want their attention focused for them. Appealing to that desire for focus in your marketing assures successful response rates.

Five Tools That Will Make You a Winner Every Time:

1. Once you've captured your prospect's attention by announcing or promoting the benefit to him, be sure you keep that attention by giving a convincing explanation of that benefit so there's no doubt in his mind that this is exactly what he needs.

2. Make a **compelling** specific offer. You can't put too much effort into this part of your marketing. Work this and rework this until it's great . . . not just good. Make a commitment to yourself to only make great offers in advertising. Remember—amaze people!

3. Establish a connection with prospects through familiarization. The best way to determine how this can be done is to use a little Focused Concentration and look at the situation through your prospect's eyes. Seeing it as he does will give you your answers. Find a way to weave a few comments into your copy that you're sure will be true with him too. This can be a feeling or need that is shared by all persons in his situation that he can relate to. The more he can relate to what you're saying, the more it shows you truly understand his needs and can fill them. This presupposes that he will be comfortable with you—a good place for you to be.

Advertising

Another way to build familiarization is through the consistent use of your photo. If you use your photo on everything, and in every flier and every ad, people will recognize your ads instantly. This recognition creates a certain familiarity. Remember: a picture is truly worth a thousand words. I think you should be honest here though. Use a reasonably current photo. The pictures of some real estate ladies amuse me. You could be waiting for them in front of a property and never recognize them when they arrive. They evidently used their high school prom picture in their ads, and they're now forty years old. What would this do to your credibility?

4. Once you've established the first two factors, you must give easy ways to contact you immediately. You've done the hard part; now just make it so easy to contact you that there's no real reason to delay.

5. Now you must create a sense of urgency—because there is. Your success! Any successful salesperson learns that if there's **any** delay—it can cost you the sale. You must close when you can close. Never delay a close in any way. The percentage of lost sales, deals, or contracts skyrockets with every passing moment of delay. Once a delay goes into days, the closing rate begins its disappearance into thin air.

There are many ways to create a sense of urgency. Usually creating a fear of loss is the best. If you recall, you read about fear of loss earlier.

My Favorite Guidelines for Great Attention Getters

- The words you use should have an announcement quality to them. A ho-hum effort here will get you a ho-hum response. Ask yourself—is this great?

- Use words like these in the beginning of your headline: "free," "why" or "which," "how to," "now or new," "at last," and any of the words in the Hot Words List.

- Attract the reader or listener through self-interest. Use the most important words in his vocabulary— "you" and "your," wherever possible.

- When possible, refer to a need or situation using a two-word headline, i.e., "Quit Smoking," "Debt Relief," or " Be Trim".

- Be sure to tell an interesting story and paint a picture. If it can be fascinating or amazing—it has the makings of a winner. I began a sales letter with a few remarks about a gypsy I met in Barcelona. People continuously refer to the gypsy story years later.

- Where applicable, include the price (or price reduction) in your headline. Even alluding to a low price or special savings can help. I've even seen outrageous prices promoted to appeal to those that need to overpay to feel a sense of status.

- Include a free or special offer. Often suggesting a special reason for the offer will motivate a prospect to action. Sometimes people need a way to justify to themselves their reason for spending money.

- Include a date in your headline, i.e., "Only Until August 1st". In many instances a fear of loss can create urgency.

- When possible, offer easily affordable, attractive payment plans. Sometimes you can break something down into segments with the first segment being exceptionally attractive. I have broken hypnotherapy classes down into three segments. The first segment being very low cost so people can experience some of the training and studies without a large commitment of time and dollars. This eliminates the need for "selling" the courses. Once people see what it's all about, it's any easy decision for them to take all the more expensive classes. This is a very fair approach and it has proven to be a strong marketing point. In almost no time at all my school strongly dominated the market in a multi-state area. Competitors now copy my marketing.

Review your headline comparing it to the Hot Words List to make sure you are satisfied with your final rendition. Then, once you're satisfied, set it aside for a day and review it again later. Don't settle for O.K. If it's not great, don't move ahead with it. Work it and rework it until you know it's great. Mediocre copy costs the same to run as great copy. Get the most for your money and effort. Remember my attorney that spends days perfecting just one letter. It saves him and his clients costly days in court over and over again.

Become a student of advertising. Start reading or at least glancing over advertising that you find at every opportunity. Know that repeats of the same ad or headline by others indicates that they are working well. Nobody keeps running

Advertising

ads that don't pull. Use what you can from them. Sometimes it takes only a little imagination to change an idea to perfectly suit your needs.

CHAPTER SIX

Love Your Junk Mail

Save your junk mail for your free time. I usually have some stashed in my car, my briefcase, and a pile ready to go whenever I think I might have some dead time between appointments. I like best to review it with scissors and have a highlighter or red pen handy. If I see something I like, I save it in my advertising idea file.

I don't just save ads. I also read all the sales letters and brochures for key phrases, and highlight them and save them in a "useful items" file. I'll save something just for a single phrase that might be useful some day.

I've always admired those people whose command of language is such that they can paint a descriptive picture with just a few words. I haven't been blessed with that ability, but I admire it so much that I save examples of it and use it. When I'm writing ad copy or sales letters, I always have my files beside me so I can draw on their ability—even though I don't have it.

Mail Advertising: Making it Work, Making it Pay

Most of the advertising principles apply in using any advertising *media* with some variations. Mail advertising still carries an attention-getting headline. It can be in the form of letters, announcements, brochures, or fliers. Many owners of private practices and small businesses have repeatedly tried mail advertising and only experienced poor results.

There are entire books devoted to the subject, but most are for businesses that rely heavily on mail advertising and have deep pockets. For most private practices and small businesses, high volume mailing is not affordable, nor is it necessary. Done correctly though, you can consider it a low cost alternative to many other advertising media. This is true if you have built a mailing list of your own. If you don't have a list yet, you can use a "host mailer."

Love Your Junk Mail

I used to mail with bookstores as the host mailer. They did their regular advertising and I had my own marketing pieces printed to accompany theirs. This is not only economical, it solves the problem of not having a list, or needing to expand yours. You can offer to share in the cost, or even the cost and the work. You'll need to seek out the right host; one that's in a complementary business yet has marketing needs similar to yours. This is another time to use your Focused Concentration to think of all the practitioners or businesses that are compatible with yours.

In the sixties and early seventies I had six real estate offices in Chicago. I had the first computer to be used in Chicago for apartment rental listings; we went through tons of preprinted computer form paper for our customer's listings. The cost of this was very high. So I contacted a furniture mover and offered to be the host for him. He paid for my forms, and I allowed him to have his advertising printed as a banner at the bottom of each page. What better place for him to have his name and phone number displayed—right in the hands of people who were moving.

A chiropractor, nutritionist, hypnotherapist, and massage therapist could work with tanning spas, beauty shops, health food stores, or health clubs for weight loss. Not only for a host/beneficiary mailing relationship, but presenting workshops and programs as well.

There's no way that I can stress enough the importance of your own mailing list. I don't share my list with anyone because it's my bread and butter. There are many things I'll share openly, but never my list. My list took years to build, and it consists of people who either know me, or have heard of me. Whenever I do a mailing to my list, the response is very high. Also, with each mailing that I do, the recipients become more familiar with me. I may become a host mailer and combine someone's literature with mine, but I don't give them my list.

Mail order marketing companies value their lists highly because they know what it costs them to build. When you see items advertised in magazines, very often the advertiser is not even expecting to make any money from the sale of the advertised item. In fact, if they can sell enough that their profits offset the cost of the ad, they're happy. They've learned that their true goal should be to get the name and address of the buyer. Now when they send ads through the mail, they know who to send them to. They also know that the advertising is going to people who know them and their products, and that they buy those types of products through the mail.

The days of running an ad and making profits directly from that ad have been over for a long, long time. Business has gone full circle. It's built by building relationships—back to just what it was in the old days. The most practical approach you can take with your advertising, is to create an opportunity to begin building new relationships. Creating that opportunity has become a process within itself.

Seven Essentials for Dynamic Sales Letters/Brochures/Fliers

1. Grab the reader's attention. *(Hot Words.)*

2. Create fear of missing out. *(Fear of loss.)*

3. Why they should believe you. *(Establish credibility/create familiarity.)*

4. Proof that it's true. *(Testimonials.)*

5. Compelling benefits. *(Why they should act now.)*

6. How to easily order. *(Simply . . . or Just . . .)*

7. Do it. *(Motivating "Do it now" instructions.)*

Use the AIDA Formula:

This well-known old formula may be helpful in remembering some of the important essentials in writing advertising copy. See if your copy conforms to these rules by containing the following:

A = **A**ttention Grabber

I = **I**nvolve Reader

D = **D**esire Creation

A = **A**ction Motivation

Checklist for Sales Letter Writing

Use this checklist when the job is just about finished; this will ensure that your copy does an exceptional job of filling all the requirements. Is it GREAT copy? Or is it just good copy? Remember, GREAT copy costs no more to run than good copy. Don't settle for less than GREAT copy from yourself. Work on it as long as it takes until it's GREAT copy.

Items should appear in this order:

Top

➤ Does it have a powerful headline?

Body

➤ Does it promote the benefits?

Body

➤ Does it convince the reader?

Body

➤ Does it eliminate the risk?

Close

➤ Does it compel the reader to act?

Stories Sell

"The best leaders—almost without exception and at every level, are master users of stories and symbols."
Tom Peters
Business Writer

I'll mention this here and again later. It's important enough to risk seeming redundant. Anytime I've been able to use an engaging story in a sales letter or flier, it's been a big success. The following true story has proven so successful that I've used it, not only in all my advertising, but in my book as well.

Here's the copy:

Dear friend,

A few years ago, through a gypsy I met while in Barcelona, Spain, I discovered the most fascinating and revealing "mind reading" technique I've ever seen. At first I thought maybe what he was showing me was gypsy "fortune telling." In just minutes I found out I was wrong, *dead wrong*. What he showed me was *serious business*. So serious that I invited him to come to the United States for a while to teach me all he knew.

What he taught me was nothing less than absolutely

incredible! So incredible, in fact, that I set out on a research mission around the world to further investigate my study of this remarkable phenomena.

Much as I suspected, this was far bigger than even my gypsy friend's wildest dreams. My research showed documented evidence of this phenomenon in England as early as 1635. Whether I was in China, Egypt, the Amazon jungle, or even Turkey, these phenomena existed and I was able to verify it everywhere in the world. This was not just a gypsy art—this was real science! Science that I was able to develop to an advanced degree. A science that I could teach.

Using what I learned, and finding that it revealed peoples' true thoughts to me, fueled my desire to learn even more. I suspected that people could be managed and manipulated by the use of this knowledge. You can imagine my surprise and amazement when further research not only proved that people *can in fact be manipulated*, they are! We are! Every day! Fortunately, the people doing the manipulating are doing it unwittingly because they're not aware of how it works.

And, of course, my next question was: "If people *knew* how this works, could they use it?" The only way to answer that question was to go out and try it . . . Just as I suspected—*it works!*

I set out like a man on a mission. The more I researched, the more I learned. Some of my discoveries gave me goose bumps so big they hurt. This not only is real; it's *powerful beyond my belief*. Many people are of the opinion that "manipulation" is improper. However, it's the intent or use that can be improper, not the knowledge and ability. In business and everyday life, this knowledge is tremendously beneficial.

Love Your Junk Mail

I'm currently in the midst of finishing my book, a complete study of this science. But, as you can imagine, a book like this takes considerable time. In the meantime, I began teaching two-day workshops on this technique with great success. Now what's happened is the workshops have taken on a life of their own. *Everyone that learns of my study wants more. Much more!*

The book will be ready next summer, but in the meantime, this is far too hot to just sit on. Too many people, and far too many corporations, can use this technique now. There's no point in waiting until my book is finished. The training manual and student workbooks are, and have been, complete for the last two years, and I've already been using them on a very limited scale. Every single person that I've trained has been awestruck by their new dimension of understanding of everybody they come in contact with. They also find that they have a new understanding of what they see and hear on the news, and in television interviews, as well as in ordinary conversations.

People are unconsciously sending you hundreds of messages from the second you meet—are you getting them?

Neuro-subliminal Communication™ goes far beyond the "body language" of the seventies. It explains away all the errors of that old study and makes your understanding multi-dimensional because it embraces new knowledge about the brain and how it operates.

People are telling you what they want, how they feel, and what they are thinking. Only those trained in this study understand even the simplest of these messages. The course consists of interactive exercises and practice, discussions, lectures, and demonstrations that will quickly move you ahead with all your professional and personal relationships.

Love Your Junk Mail

You'll become a tougher customer because you'll know what sales people are thinking. You'll be amazed and delighted at your ability to decipher messages people are sending you about their likes and dislikes, how they really feel about you, when they will be receptive towards you, and a host of other unbelievable secrets. The presenter will also touch on the origin of these signals and why you can rely on them.

Whether dealing in business, with clients, or even your love interest, possession of this knowledge can be the key to your success.

You will learn how to:

Make people like you instantly.
Make people see things your way.
Make people magically want to cooperate with you.
Test for acceptance of your suggestions before they're offered.
Communicate subconsciously to get much more "inside" meaning from every conversation.
Make people want to give you your way.
Avoid being manipulated—subconsciously!
How your actions can be predicted . . . before you're aware of them yourself!

Answers to these questions:

Is he lying?
Does she like me?
Do they believe me?
Can I trust her?
Is this the right price?
Do they really agree?

Love Your Junk Mail

Is my timing correct?
Do they trust me?
Is he/she attracted to me?
Will the answer be yes or no?
Who's picking up the check?

You need these answers every day when: buying a car,
buying a house, meeting new friends, committing to others,
relating to your love, giving your trust, communicating with
co-workers, and raising children.

My time is limited to teaching this course only once every
three or four months. Early in 1999, I launched a certified
trainer program for N-s C, authorizing trained persons to
teach this course to individuals, groups, companies, and large
corporations. The information in this course is *very much in
demand*, so this will be an excellent business opportunity for
certified trainers.

This will be a complete program with courses taught
internationally in many languages. I already have trainers
lined up for Polish, Spanish, and French. The Leidecker
Institute will provide ongoing support, and graduates taught
by the trainers will receive, from the Institute, certification as
a N-sC technician. This certification will be an excellent
addition to the graduate's resume for career enhancement in
their respective fields.

This upcoming course presents an important opportunity for
you, whether you wish to apply later for the certified trainer
training as a career or business opportunity, or if you simply
want the power of this knowledge for your own personal use
in improving your lot in life.

To enroll, simply call 847-844-1933. Why not call now?

Love Your Junk Mail

Yours truly,

Arthur A. Leidecker, BCH

CHAPTER SEVEN

Counteract Procrastination

People tend to procrastinate and then forget to act, or lose motivation. What may seem like a great idea when someone first reads your letter or ad, may not seem nearly as appealing later. The more successful you are in getting them to act immediately, the more successful your advertising will be. Studies show that with each passing day, advertising response drops dramatically. In any kind of sales, **the time to close is right now!** You can make a special offer to those who respond within the next "X" number of days. Give them a strong reason to act right now. Often a bonus for prompt action will do the trick. It's best if the bonus is something you can economically produce yourself, like a special report or booklet. You may even be able to find an appropriate item that you can buy wholesale at low cost.

Coupons and Certificates

I personally don't like to use the word "coupon." To me a "certificate" sounds so much more sophisticated or valuable. Since it doesn't cost any more, why not consider using certificates for a promotion? They're great motivators as a call to action if you give them an expiration date. I like to create certificates that look very impressive and valuable. I don't want them to even look like a coupon.

I have three pet peeves about coupons used by some companies. It may just be a personal peculiarity, but I think they're worth considering. The first one is: making the customer using the coupon feel like a second-class citizen for using it. I can't understand the mentality in offering a deal to attract customers and then treating them less than first-class for accepting your offer.

The second is: having hidden little "gotchas" in the fine print that severely restrict the use of the coupon. The last time I got caught by a gotcha, the business owner grinned as he showed me where it said my coupon was no good that day. I told him he was right—he fooled me. But now because he cleverly fooled me, I wasn't going to do business with him—ever!

And here's the third: coupons that say, "First time customers only!" To me this is just like slapping your longtime loyal customers in the face. It's like telling them you have no regard for them. I believe that if you can't afford to make an offer, don't make it. Wouldn't it be nice to say, "New customers, and loyal past customers too?"

Typos –The Credibility Thief

ALWAYS have "fresh eyes" proofread your copy whether it's ads, letters, or brochures. No matter how hard you try, you can't effectively proofread your own writing. The problem is that your subconscious mind knows what you're trying to say, and reads the copy as its supposed to appear— not as it actually does. No matter who the writer, proofreader, publisher, or printer is, it is becoming increasingly difficult to eliminate typos from your work. Part of this can be blamed on the use of spellcheckers in most software programs. They can find misspelled words, but can't usually pick out misplaced words. Unfortunately, typos do affect your credibility. It pays to work very hard and make every effort to eliminate them.

It especially pays to have fresh eyes do your copy proofreading if they're totally unfamiliar with your service or product. The less familiar, so much the better; they don't know what it's supposed to say, so they won't unconsciously read corrections into your work as they're reading.

How Much To Spend On Advertising?

Ideally you want to spend as much as necessary, but not a dime more than you have to. The good news is that if you don't have much of an advertising budget, you can replace spending dollars with spending energy. I've found that spending energy brings a higher return, and has a more enduring impact than spending dollars anyway. In most instances, once the ad is run and the money spent, within a few short days the impact has subsided. But whenever you properly invest your energy, that impact lives longer— sometimes it even takes on a life of its own. We'll cover energy vs. dollars in more detail later.

Theoretically, you could spend $400 to advertise and service a client that brought in $500 since that would provide a $100 profit. Now your first inclination might be to say, "Well that's not hardly worth it." But, if you spent $4000, that would be a $1000 profit. And, if you could do it more often, the profits would multiply.

The idea is to determine the amount needed without spending any more than necessary. This requires that you keep good records. Only invest heavily in advertising that you know works.

Testing

"Chance favors the prepared mind."
Louis Pasteur (1822—1895)
Chemist

Try various methods of advertising pieces and print them in small quantities, marking each in some way to determine which is most successful. You will be tempted to just get started and not be that patient in waiting for results, but rushing this can cost you heavily. Plan your marketing well enough in advance to allow time for testing. Long range planning pays dividends, and if you run out of funds you'll wish you slowed down enough to test. It's better to find out a piece of advertising is a bomb in small quantities, than after you've spent a few thousand dollars on a mail campaign that flops.

I've always encouraged this in my marketing workshops to save people from wasting money on an idea that doesn't fly. Then the day came where I discovered another good reason for testing: your advertising could be too successful! You may find the response so overwhelming that you can't handle all the extra business properly.

Hypnotists can't legally re-tape copyrighted music for client use. They use royalty free background music for taping scripts for clients for specific purposes. This music can cost them as much as four hundred dollars per copy. I created some hypnotic music with a new software program on my computer and named it *Astral Journey.* I sent out the following letter in a test mailing of two hundred pieces. You'll note that the letter has a "story" quality to it. This is an important ingredient in any sales letter you mail out. Remember this important advertising detail: **Stories sell.** This letter brought so many responses that we couldn't keep up with the calls for two days after they were delivered. From the initial mailing of only two hundred letters, we even got a call from Australia where a hypnotist talking to a friend heard about the deal. Not only that, we could barely keep up with the duplicating of tapes.

Here's the letter:

Dear Fellow Hypnotist,

I've used the same royalty-free music for years. Not because I particularly liked it so much, but because I couldn't find anything more suitable than what I had—and I've tried. I've looked at every convention I attended, bought what was available for various high prices, and still couldn't find what I was looking for.

I even went so far as to investigate having my own music composed. Four hundred dollars was the most reasonable price I could find, and there was no guarantee that it would be exactly what I wanted.

Recently, I got a brochure in the mail for some music that sounded like it might just fill the bill. It was only $49.95 plus $5.00 shipping and handling. I sent off for it right away. Within five minutes after receiving it I knew the composer was not a hypnotist, nor did he even consult one. His music consisted of all the unusual tricks and sounds his electronic system could produce. He unfortunately gave it "his all." The result was a demonstration of "musical gymnastics"—not nearly relaxing enough for hypnosis.

Finally, after investing over four thousand dollars in a special computer and software, I found a way to create music that has real value—music that's **especially good for deep trance work and regressions**. The big plus is that since I created the music myself on my computer and named it *Astral Journey*, there's no composer or musician to pay. I'm offering this 1 ½ hour-long tape for only $20.00, or on CD for $35.00, **including shipping and handling.**

Why so cheap you might ask? The answer is simple. If you get real value for your $20.00, you'll look favorably on the Leidecker Institute, and possibly look to us in the future when you're interested in the new light and sound technology we offer for hypnotists.

That's it—plain and simple. For $20.00 you can copy and sell all the copies of this tape you want and put all the profits in your pocket.

And believe it or not, I'll even guarantee that you'll like the tape or I'll send your money back and you won't even have to mail the tape back to me. Is that dumb? I hope not. I'm trusting that most people in our profession are honest, and I'm confident you'll like *Astral Journey*.

So grab your credit card and give us a call. We'll send your tape or CD out in the next mail.

Sincerely,

Arthur A. Leidecker, BCH

30,000 Gallons of fruit drink

Action but no sales? If you've got lots of activity but no sales, don't panic! You're halfway there. The hardest part is done. I have never seen action that cannot be turned into dollars. And, of course, that brings to mind another story to illustrate my point.

During one of those tough times when I had to start all over again, I was looking for ways to generate more dollars than a typical salary was likely to provide.

I had made the acquaintance of a man that had a huge jelly factory. He had purchased a fruit drink bottling company at an auction and moved it into his jelly factory, expecting to also produce fruit drinks that his food brokers could market along with the jellies.

He produced 30,000 gallon jugs of juice, stockpiled them in his facility, and then found out the products were incompatible. The spores of yeast floating around in the air of the jelly factory shortened the shelf-life of the 30,000 gallons of fruit drink. If he held on to them, they would all begin to ferment.

He asked me if I had any ideas. Since I was looking to accumulate enough cash to get back into a business of some sort, I told him if he sold me the fruit drinks on credit for 50 cents for a two and a half gallon jug, and loaned me a truck, I'd take them to the flea market and see what I could do.

He loaned me a big truck, and his warehousemen loaded on eight hundred of the two and a half gallon jugs. Out of curiosity, we also added a small load of jellies and apple butter. Off I went to the flea market for an afternoon of selling. I set up shop and waited for the action to start. People looked—but they weren't buying. Everyone kept coming over to me asking about all the colorful jugs, but they weren't buying. After a half an hour of only a few sales, I realized I was going to have to unload all these jugs myself by hand when I returned them. I decided that instead of taking them all back, I would lower my price and try to sell them for $2.50 instead of the $3.00 I was asking. The other problem now was, everyone already knew the higher price. How was I going to get the word out that the price was reduced?

The thought of unloading all those jugs motivated me to get over any thoughts of shyness. I got up on the tailgate of the truck and began shouting, "C'mon everybody, I don't want to have to take all this stuff back. Get 'em now before I leave. Get a free jar of jelly or apple butter with every two jugs of fruit drink." I sold out the truckload by the end of the day, returned the truck, and put $800 in my pocket for an afternoon's work. (This was in the early 70's when $800 was a very good day's pay.)

The point is, if you have created a lot of activity or interest without sales, don't panic. You're probably sitting right on top of success. Try different techniques until you succeed. Don't give up at the first obstacle.

Once, I started advertising in a local magazine that I had been told by several people was no good. One owner of a practice told me that the readers of that publication were either broke or dreamers. He said that he got a lot of calls from his ads but that they were useless. I immediately increased the size of my ads. I knew that if he was getting a lot of calls on his ads, the business was there. One only needs to find out how to successfully handle those calls.

Counteract Procrastination

My ads brought a lot of calls. I tried different responses to the callers and finally learned exactly how to handle them. Now, any competitors that want to advertise can copy some of my ad copy, but they'll have to figure out the next step. For the last several years, and to this day, I run two full-page ads in that "lousy magazine."

CHAPTER EIGHT

Free Advertising

Press releases are free but take energy (energy vs. dollars). There's really no magic to them, but getting them printed or aired can be an art. The following guidelines will help you get them accepted. Find out what a magazine's editorial deadline is and adhere to it. Call and ask for a copy of their editorial guidelines and follow them carefully. No one wants to do your work for you. Human nature is such, that if all things are equal, the neater and better prepared press release will be used.

Free Advertising

Newspapers have shorter deadlines, but special feature sections usually are considered somewhat earlier.

Skip the cover letter. They don't want to read them. Put your press release on your letterhead so they have all the pertinent information, i.e., name, phone, and address on the same document.

You may include a cover letter if it's a personal invitation to a special event that they might want to attend. (Be realistic about this.)

Always include an interesting, quality photo. The photo must tell a story about the topic. Don't send a posed, boring shot. The photo has to be interesting enough to make someone want to read the copy.

A well-written headline and an interesting photo may keep your press release out of the paper shredder.

According to editors, here are ten of the biggest reasons your press release might not be used.

1. They're poorly written. The editor does not have the time or interest to rewrite a poorly written press release.

2. The topic is not appropriate for their publication. Don't waste your time sending press releases to all the publications on a list. Be selective.

3. The press release does not contain enough information. The editor is not likely to call you for needed information; he'll just pass your press release by and print another.

Free Advertising

4. The information you've sent is old news or too close to the editorial date. Be sure you've allowed enough lead time to get your press release considered.

5. Your information is too technical for their readers. Don't fall victim of "personal reference criteria," where you assume everyone knows what you know.

6. Your press release is too long. Again, the editor won't take time to rewrite your press release for you.

7. Your press release sounds like advertising copy. Remember, this is a public interest topic—not an ad.

8. Your press release is not interesting. Write and rewrite your press release until you're sure it will be interesting to others.

9. Your writing style is inappropriate for their publication. If they're formal, you should be formal—if they're informal, be the same.

10. Your photographs are poor. Work and time is the real issue here as it is in most reasons for rejection. The editor will not take the time, or make the effort to call you for a better photo. He'll just skip your release. If you're not sure of your photo, send a couple of choices for his review.

More Free Advertising

The easiest way to get more free advertising is to write an article. Magazines and newspapers are always looking for material. Don't be disappointed if your first few offers aren't accepted. This is worthwhile enough to pursue and be persistent. Many magazines and periodicals will instruct you as to the format that suits them. You can then send the article on a disk, or upload it to them.

If you're intimidated by the thought of writing an article, start with a short report that you can offer for free at events, trade shows, or at any other opportunity. After doing this for awhile, you can expand your reports and run ads offering a free report.

By the time you're writing reports well enough to advertise them, they should be at least 18 to 20 pages long to be perceived as valuable. If you don't want to write one yourself, you can tape it on a recorder and pay a service or find a friend to transcribe it for you. In my opinion, you should discipline yourself to learn to do it. If you can talk, you can write. (Later, when I cover workshops and seminars, I'll explain a system I use that will help your report "fall together.")

Seven-Second Presentations

Often, it's not easy to just strike up a conversation about what you do with just anyone you might meet. For example: Do you promote your business when you pay at the fast food drive-up window? Do you consistently promote your business to the sales clerk when you make a purchase? You should, and you can—and it should only take no more than seven-seconds.

This is another time to use your Focused Concentration to come up with a creative idea. I found some individually wrapped Lifesaver candies and bought several bags of them. Then I printed up a quantity of postcard size fliers on heavy cardstock and stapled a piece of candy to the upper right hand corner of each card. Printed on the card it said: "Learning how to promote your practice can be a real lifesaver." At the bottom I had the details of an upcoming marketing class I was doing.

An item like this provides a quick way to give a short sales pitch without sounding pushy or opportunistic. You can develop your own creative gadget or gimmick with an appropriate opening line, or find something useful and clever in an advertising specialties catalog. Of course, you can get by very economically if you create your own. My Lifesaver candy cards cost me mere pennies apiece.

At one hypnotist's convention, I was placing my Lifesaver cards everywhere in the hotel lobby and meeting rooms. I soon realized that someone was going around and pulling the candy off the cards and leaving them. At first I was dismayed. Then someone told me about the two hypnotists who were boasting to all who would listen, about how they were so smart in getting all the free candy. What more could I ask for? I continued putting out the cards for them to steal the candy. They continued to keep my cards and my name in everyone's mind throughout the weekend as they bragged. They'll probably read this book—thanks guys!

Seven-second presentations are a fun and very productive way to be prospecting for clients everywhere you go. It's also a good way to always be "in" the business, rather than just "doing" the business.

I've had "Things to do" tablets printed. The tablets are another inexpensive and popular handout that you can give to anyone enabling you to open a conversation.

When doing a seven-second presentation, a good way to explain what you do when asked is: "Have you ever wanted to give someone a very special one of a kind gift? Well, I create heirloom quality portraits." Or, "Do you know people that have incredibly stressful lives? Well, I solve that problem for them by teaching them stress management." Or, "Do you know people that are miserable because they're afflicted by unexplained problems? Well, I help by teaching them a holistic approach to healthy living."

Your business cards, however, are not suitable for a seven-second presentation. I see business cards all the time that are mini billboards. They're crammed with so much information that one would be discouraged from reading them. They shout at a reader hungrily announcing their owner's desperation in attempting to market their business. Business cards are not an advertising medium. Don't expect them to do your job.

Your business card should be a tasteful way of simply stating your profession and how to contact or find you. Nothing more! You can't do a decent job marketing yourself or your products on a business card, so why make them look unprofessional with nothing to be gained. My belief is that a prospect should be very interested or sold by the time you are giving them your card.

A nice touch that I discovered while working with the movie companies was to write my home phone number on my card as I gave it to a movie executive. I didn't have it printed on them because that would indicate that I gave it to everyone. By making an issue of writing my home number on my card as I gave it to them, it implied that I thought them to be important. This may or may not be appropriate in your business or practice—a decision you'll have to consider.

Fliers, Posters, and Brochures

If you have a personal computer, or access to one, you're in great shape. You can create your own marketing literature. If you don't, you can lay it out yourself and have it typeset at one of the stationery super stores or by a secretarial service that does a little graphics. Most all of these services will work on a price per page basis.

To save dollars and time, lay out your work, have it typeset, buy special papers, and have the typesetting copied onto your special papers for a professional look. Set your copy up in a way that will allow you to easily change the dates and address of your event or promotion. Once your copy has been typeset, you can make several "masters." Make these master copies by merely pasting blank paper over the date and location and having copies of that printed. Each time you run that program or event again, you'll be able to create a new "camera ready" master copy by inserting the new dates and locations in the blank masters you've made.

If you're on a brutally tight budget, you can "spiff up" plain white paper by taping several high liters together and putting a rainbow swipe on the corner or some other interesting place on your flyer. This is good in a time pinch or when you don't want to invest much money in a particular flyer. The rainbow will make your copy sparkle and look very "artsy."

To get the maximum value out of all your fliers and posters, always prominently say: "Bring a friend" somewhere in the copy. It costs you nothing to say this, and it will cause many people to not only bring someone, but may also give some prospects that wouldn't have considered attending, an idea for a good time with a friend. It'll add to your attendance.

Tear-off Posters

Tear-off posters are small posters printed on letter size paper that have a number of tear-off tabs with the response phone number printed on them. Usually the tabs are snipped along the sides for easy removal of each tab. A reader simply tears off the tab and then has the necessary phone number to respond. It's a good idea to tear off the first two tabs to give the impression that others are interested. Many people simply don't want to be first or be independent; they feel more comfortable doing what others are doing.

Tear-off posters work well in stores, on bulletin boards in supermarkets, and in large office building lunch or coffee rooms (usually found in basements or first floors). Set up a route, and every few days go around and replace the posters where needed. Many store managers or "bulletin board police" will remove your bulletins. Don't take it personally. Just keep replacing them. If you get a phone complaint, just apologize and explain to them that you just thought that they were interested in community good will, but if they would like, you'll take them down. Then, also ask for their name again and the proper spelling. Often, the bulletin board police are very officious, self-appointed and acting on their own. When questioned in detail, they withdraw their complaint and grant permission, as they don't want to be responsible for making a bad decision.

Three-Up Fliers

Three-up fliers are a very economical way of advertising. Lay out your work in landscape format (which is with the longest measurement running left to right). Have it printed or copied repeating the copy vertically three times side by side, cut it into individual fliers, and distribute.

If your budget is tight, you can have the fliers copied on inexpensive white paper, put a colorful rainbow on them, and cut them yourself in your spare time while watching TV.

If you're advertising an event or promotion (notice I didn't say your business—always an event or something specific), it's good to have posters and three-up fliers for placing on stores' countertops. When you set up your poster route you can do fliers at the same time. I often did all three—posters, fliers, and brochures. I want a supply of brochures for people that call for information anyway.

Don't sell these methods short. If they seem inappropriate for your business, you may not be thinking of the appropriate approach or type of locations for them (i.e., proper type of shops, right quality paper, print style, colors, etc.), And don't forget . . . They must be headed with a strong "what's in it for them" headline—not your name or your business's name.

Free Advertising

When you're out checking on your supply of brochures or fliers at the locations you've placed them, take a minute and tidy up the spot. Storeowners usually are displaying these things as a community public service. They consider having to keep organizing the brochure display a thankless chore; often it's the last thing to get done. If you'll take a moment to tidy up the display, a couple things happen: your brochures look better, the whole display looks more appealing, thus helping you, and the store owner appreciates you and knows you appreciate them. On one occasion, I went into a bookstore to place brochures and there was no room. I always took care of the display in this store, cleaning, organizing, and tidying up so I didn't feel I was asking too much of the store owner to put out my brochures when space became available. The storeowner said, "There's always space available for you," as she threw someone else's brochures in the garbage. "Put your brochures here." I'm not advocating throwing people's brochures in the garbage, but it's a good example of how much a storeowner might appreciate your efforts.

Sources for specialty papers: **Quill: 1-800-789-1331** and **Paper Direct: 1-800-272-7377**. Call them for a free catalog. I have often found what I want at **Staples** or **Office Depot** as well.

CHAPTER NINE

Host Beneficiary Relationships

This is like having as many hardworking partners as you can set up. Look for companies that are non-competitive but do a business with the same type of people that could use your services as well. It can be something that complements their business by bringing in more clients or by offering a service or product their clients want and need.

When you can create a relationship like this, you reap the benefits of all their advertising for free.

Host Beneficiary Relationships

I have a relationship like this with the Elgin, Illinois Park District. They are always looking for adult education programs for their residents. I have also had them with several bookstores. Elgin gives me a large free ad in their activities catalog which is widely distributed. They collect the money, provide the room, handle all the calls, answer all the questions, and give me a printed roster when I walk in to do the workshop. I just present the workshop and send them an invoice. This host beneficiary relationship has now grown into a series of courses at Elgin Community College.

Browsing the yellow pages is a great place to find ideas for hosts. Before approaching prospective hosts, carefully plan how they could benefit from the relationship.

Offer your prospective host a commission or referral fee where practical. In some cases, you may want to offer your customer list.

You can also be a host by doing the same thing in reverse, receiving a referral fee from successful referrals.

Can you think of any possible situations?

How about

- Beauty shops

- Health clubs

- Book stores

Host Beneficiary Relationships

- Health food stores

- Tanning spas

- Gift shops

- Libraries

- Any business where their customers or clients would need your services if they use the host's services or products. Of course this would be a non-competitive business.

In some cases, you may do some joint venturing with another business for an event or an ongoing joint venture while still maintaining your own business and identity.

> *"Roadblock's aren't barriers—they open your eyes to other routes."*
> *Joyce Restaino*
> *Writer*

Don't give up if you get a few refusals or run into some rejection. Don't take the rejection personally, and don't accept other people's negative opinions as a reason to feel less valuable than you are. Many people have personal problems that have nothing to do with your proposal.

Host Beneficiary Relationships

Consider these estimates of American problems:

- 12,000,000 Americans are alcoholic or on drugs. That means 10% of their spouses or significant others are neurotic to a varying degree—which means their offspring are dysfunctionally neurotic. Averaging two children per couple, that equals 2,400,000 neurotic children and 1,200,000 neurotic spouses.

- 5% have other emotional problems.

- 20% are fearful of their future. (48% express fears over their job security.)

- 5% are ill.

- 50% get divorced. (More than 5% want to.)

- 30% are overweight and struggling with their own self-esteem.

- 1,000,000 will have a heart attack this year.

- 25,000,000 will suffer with high blood pressure.

- 8,000,000 have stomach ulcers.

- 230,000,000 prescriptions for tranquilizers will be filled.

- 57% of adults are frustrated with new technology.

- 5,000,000 suffer a testosterone deficiency.

- 30,000,000 suffer from cardiovascular disease.

Host Beneficiary Relationships

People's poor regard for you probably has nothing to do with you at all—they're just tangled in a web of their own dilemmas.

Should you allow them to measure your worth? Not hardly . . . better you judge your worth yourself, and should they reject you, try to have a little sympathy for them; they may be one of the above statistics. When everything is going well in a person's world, or if they're well balanced, they're nice to others. Unkindness on people's part is often their own lack of self-actualization expressing itself.

Just one or two host beneficiary arrangements can enhance your income considerably—so persevere. It pays to work hard at setting a few up.

CHAPTER TEN

Revenue Streams

Referrals—The Heart Of Your Business

Everyone wants to know the magic behind getting lots of referrals. More than half of my business consistently comes from referrals. I've always gotten a lot, however, I wanted to analyze exactly what it is that I've been doing that has worked so well. I used a Focused Concentration session looking for the answer and found out that: **there is no magic**. But, the simplicity of getting lots of referrals is so elementary it's overlooked by most people while they are on a quest for a sophisticated discovery. I thought back to my experience in working with large numbers of Polish immigrants in one of my businesses. They were incredibly resourceful, and knew where to get the best buys for their dollar in just about any product or service they needed. They never went to the phone directory, newspaper advertising, or TV ads for their answers—they networked.

I also thought back to my travel in foreign countries. What was the best way to find my way around? The best sights, the best restaurants, and the best experiences were not the ones found in guidebooks or ads; they were found by asking other tourists what they knew or experienced that was good.

That's exactly how referrals will come to you—from people that know you, or know of you by hearing good things about you. The key words then are: **positive exposure**. Throughout this book there are methods and suggestions for you to get the exposure you need. Fortunately, they don't necessarily require much money either. They will, however, require an expenditure of energy. You'll almost always find the opportunity to opt to replace spending money with spending energy. In fact, usually the results you have gained spending energy endure long after the expensive advertising is forgotten. I've had people come to me years after they got my name from a satisfied client. So if you want referrals, choose the methods to get exposure that suit you, and do as much of it as you possibly can. I see no easier, softer way.

Do you have a referral program? It doesn't have to be a sophisticated program where you give certain things for referrals, but it should at least be a routine you faithfully follow. Have thank you cards or a prewritten letter on hand and an established routine where people giving you referrals are always thanked whether or not the referral becomes actual business.

Revenue Streams

If in your practice, however, it is practical and appropriate to give rewards for referrals, consider this: Referral programs don't cost as much as advertising because you only give something in return for a new client. You're not spending only in hopes of gaining new clients. It's best if you can reward referrals with a credit towards your services or products. This way they get a larger dollar value with lower cost to you, and it gives you an opportunity for more business.

In many professional settings a referral is only rewarded with a thank you, and it may be inappropriate to offer more. Seek local advice on this if you're not sure.

Real estate agents have long known the importance of referrals. They even have stickers with little red hearts that say "I love referrals." Ask your local agent to get some for you. The cost is nominal. You can also easily print thank you stickers on your home computer. I have them placed on every piece of mail and merchandise shipment that goes out of my office; except mail to first time inquiries.

Every one of my large magazine ads has a little service mark in the lower left corner that says: "All referrals valued and appreciated."

Since so much good business comes from referrals, doesn't it make sense to create a plan or a program that encourages people to refer clients to you?

Six Steps to More Referrals

1. Ask customers for referrals.

2. Offer a gift, discount, premium, or credit towards a purchase.

3. Ask other businesses to recommend your services.

4. Offer special incentives for referrals for holidays and special occasions.

5. Offer deals to companies that send referrals.

6. Promptly thank them for every referral.

Customer Loyalty

Communicate regularly with your clients shortly after their first business with you. Establish special programs for your better clients and give them special attention. You can send them more personal notes or a token gift, and ask how you may better serve them.

You can spend a lot of money to acquire new clients; however, it doesn't cost nearly as much to keep cyrrent clients and continue to enjoy business from them.

Send a holiday letter instead of a card. Wish your client and their family joy filled holidays and a happy New Year, and thank them for their business through the year in an

128

appropriate way. This letter should be more personal in tone, and might tell a little about you and your family.

Regaining Clients

Many times the loss of a client has nothing to do with you or your service. They just don't get back to you for one reason or another, and then fall out of touch or the habit.

Re-establish contact by phone or mail and express your concern that all is well with them, and inquire if there is anything you could be doing for them. If there was a problem with your service, this is your opportunity to rectify it.

Strengthen ties with clients at every opportunity and let them know that you value them.

One great way to do almost all of these things is through a regular newsletter. Initially, this may seem like a lot of work, but it soon becomes easier. You can provide a real service to all your clients/customers by keeping them informed about issues relating to your profession that could affect them. Be sure your newsletter does not appear to be *only* a self-serving ad sheet.

A chiropractor could produce a health newsletter rather than a letter on just chiropractic. This would keep the newsletter interesting and make it easier to provide new information on a frequent basis.

Revenue Streams

Some businesses might require more creativity in newsletters than others, and some newsletters might, out of necessity, be just one short page long. But even a very short newsletter is still an economical opportunity to maintain contact with your customers and prospects. They might be sent out at the right time to be in your client's thoughts, i.e. Christmas, Easter, Mothers Day, springtime, etc.

Selling More

While the quest for more new clients should be ongoing, an immediate source of additional revenue, at no additional expense, can be from your existing client/customer base. Most likely you'll find your clients will be better served by providing them with additional services and products.

My practice basically consists of teaching hypnotherapy. My students will need many things when they start their practice. Usually, not only don't they know what they need, they have no idea where to get it. I have the following available for them: special music to use for hypnosis; three different hypnotherapy script manuals; high tech light and sound equipment; frequent advanced learning workshops they can attend; and, I carry a complete catalog of Nightingale-Conant audio and videotape albums.

Students appreciate the convenience of having these items available to them, and often contact me after their classes for additional purchases. Some fellow hypnotherapy instructors say they don't want to "fool around" with these things, yet they will spend a great deal of time hunting and shopping endlessly for a cheaper hotel in which to hold their classes.

Revenue Streams

It's nice to offset that expense by offering additional items to my students and continue holding classes in a better hotel for the few extra dollars.

I don't "sell" these items. I only have them available.

I present weight management workshops, and always have self-hypnosis music audiocassettes available for participants. I never "sell" them; I just have a small quantity of them available on the table. Invariably, almost every participant buys one.

I just completed writing a small book that ties in with my weight management program, combining it with light and sound machines. I'll put them together with tapes; thereby making a nice weight management package for program attendees to continue on their own after the workshop has concluded.

A psychologist from Milwaukee, Wisconsin that I trained in hypnotherapy, was invited by a hospital to conduct a guided imagery workshop for psychologists from his area. While the hospital was only offering him one hundred and fifty dollars for his daylong presentation, he agreed to do it to gain the professional exposure. Just as I had a display when he attended class, he had a quantity of nice, copyright-free tapes made to offer for sale.

Each tape cost him less than a dollar to make. Upon the completion of his workshop, he **merely mentioned** that he had tapes of the music he used available. End result—he sold out of tapes earning far more than the workshop fees he collected.

Audiocassette programs are not an "easy-sell" retail item, but if you're presenting a good program, they will sell themselves at the presentation. Of course, the same holds true for books or reports written by you.

You can create "add-ons" by offering appropriate items or services to a client at a special, lower price. A portrait photographer in my workshop began her line with a standard frame and then offered several deluxe frames. A special price is given on the top-of-the-line frames when an additional portrait is commissioned, such as: an additional portrait of another family member, or another copy of the original portrait to use as a gift.

Add-ons can often be a related item that a client will want, which ties in nicely with what you're doing or providing for him. If you think this through carefully with Focused Concentration, you'll most likely come up with an item, or items, that you create or produce yourself. This could be an instructional or informational audiocassette, a booklet containing instructions, or a special report you've created.

"Bundling"

Bundling is the packaging of several items or services to increase the sales volume of an individual sale. The fast food chains do it with a combination of a sandwich, fries, and a drink. They do it because they have found that we may not order a large fries, or a large drink, but since it's conveniently included—why not? Bridal shops do it. Catering services do it. Auto manufacturers do it with option packages. And undertakers do it with funeral and casket purchases. Even carwashes do it.

Revenue Streams

You may have to get creative to implement it, but why should you miss out?

When I see clients I have them agree to a minimum package of three sessions after which we'll evaluate their progress. I explain that during those three sessions I will be teaching them self-hypnosis so they won't have to be dependant on me for reinforcement. I also explain that self-hypnosis is something they will learn and can use the rest of their lives. This makes good sense, and I have no problem with clients not wanting three sessions. To prevent the occurrence of "no-shows," I immediately, upon booking an appointment, send a confirming letter accompanied by a client intake form and a self-addressed envelope. To further prevent no-shows, I will not set appointments any sooner than three weeks in advance (it usually takes at least that anyway). The day before the appointment the client receives a confirming call.

The way what I've just described to you comes together is as follows: when the client asks about the sessions, I explain that I only see clients for a minimum of three sessions, and before an objection or question about the number of sessions can develop, I explain the good reason why. I do the same when I explain the cost per session. I tell them that it's one hundred twenty-five dollars a session, and before they form a question about the cost, I explain that the first session is one and a half hours long and that there's no extra charge for the extra time. I then advise them the earliest I can see them is in three weeks. People perceive value in things they must wait for. I do not have no-shows.

Additional Revenue Streams

Whatever marketing system produces best for you should be continued, but you should test other methods. Find other ways to market your services. Don't stop once you've found a method that works. That method may stop working or become impractical at some point. Not only that, you may find access to an entirely new customer base through a new marketing medium or system. You also want to create other services you can provide. In my case, there are only so many people interested in becoming hypnotherapists in any given month. For that reason, I've created several other related classes. Once I've enrolled them in **all** my classes, there's no more I can do in that area.

I keep creating additional products to offer: light and sound machines, writing my own books, and producing tapes. Due to the fluctuation in client and customer buying habits, you may need to come up with something to create additional revenue streams. Do this to maintain a more even cash flow. This is an excellent opportunity to practice and derive real value from practicing Focused Concentration to come up with additional revenue streams. Don't forget—this is time well invested, because just one good idea can pay you well for the rest of your life.

Later on in my business, I invested in professional grade video equipment and began selling my courses via the Internet throughout the U.S. and in foreign countries. Why not? I'm already spending the time teaching the classes—why not tape them and offer them worldwide? It only takes a small amount of time to answer questions and keep up with my distance students via e-mail. Students then fly to Chicago from all over the world to meet their minimum in-person, class-time requirements. The Internet has taken my business worldwide with a reasonable amount of effort and expense.

Now, due to the cost of coming to Chicago, renting a car, and the inconvenience of driving in a foreign country, I've created a new program. Students can simply fly into a port city and take their in-person training on a cruise. The actual cost is comparable to the costs of staying in a hotel, renting a car, and eating all their meals in a restaurant. A big plus is they all are conveniently in class, well fed, and on time while they enjoy a luxurious cruise. I have the enjoyable task of teaching classes to students from a market that I would ordinarily never have reached. (On a tax deductible, all expense paid cruise.)

"Scalloping"

Soap manufacturers use scalloping to "perk up" a product that has become stale when its sales have dropped off. They'll add something, or alter a product in some way and come out with the "new and improved" version of an old product that has become ho-hum.

I've done that with past life regression workshops (a form of hypnotherapy). I added aromatherapy and the element of high-tech light and sound to them, and called them "sensualized" past life regressions. Because I incorporated the involvement of more senses, it adds a dimension of "new and improved" to what was a hot item anyway, but has been around a long time and needed a fresh advertising approach.

CHAPTER ELEVEN

Your Niche

In most professional practices and many businesses, you don't need to struggle with the task of wresting clients from a competitor's grasp. It's important to evaluate your particular situation. Your need may be more to educate people about the services you offer and what you can do for them. If that's the case, your marketing may need an altogether different approach. You may need to get information out, rather than show why "your's" is better. This can be a real deciding factor in where, what, and how much you spend in your business. It can even be a determining factor in the language in your advertising copy. Give some careful thought to what your marketing challenge is: competing—or educating. Without careful consideration of this factor, you could find yourself spending your efforts and dollars the wrong way.

Building Your Practice or Business With Free Community Education Seminars and Workshops

No matter what type of practice you have or business you're in, you can offer a community education seminar or workshop. I don't know of an easier or more economical way to establish yourself as an authority in your field. Just as I said earlier, "Would you rather call a heating man for your furnace repair, or would you rather call the guy that wrote a book on furnace repair?" The same answer holds true with establishing yourself as an authority in presenting workshops or community education seminars.

Would you rather hire just an attorney—or would you rather hire an attorney that teaches and is also an author?

Would you like to consult with a dermatologist—or a dermatologist that teaches seminars or wrote a book on skin problems.

Would you rather go to a photographer—or a portrait photographer that teaches a workshop on how to take good photos.

Your Niche

The point is: practically anything you do can be taught in a workshop or seminar.

The Madison Avenue folks know that people want to gain significance. Most people don't know how to do this, so Madison Avenue convinces them that they can do it for them. They work very hard at creating the perception in the minds of the public that they can achieve status by overpaying, or buying a popular brand name, or more overpriced quality than they need.

Remember, you can gain the significance that others pay a fortune for by presenting workshops and seminars that establish you as an authority in your field. It's not important whether your events are very well attended or not. Most likely in the very beginning, the attendance will not be as large as you'd like. Don't let that deter you. Just the fact that you conduct one is success. Once you do, you can refer to your seminar in conversation and in marketing pieces. You are now a teacher. If you do this on a steady basis, your attendance will grow. Many people will need be invited several times before they finally get around to attending. I have students attend my classes that have been thinking about it for three and four years before they finally enroll.

When I retired and decided I wanted to start practicing hypnotherapy, I did not want to spend years to build a practice. I wanted it to grow quickly and didn't want to spend a fortune to get there. First, I tested the market and marketing techniques to find out what it was going to take, and where to spend my energy and dollars.

I ran a few ads to see what the response would be and plot my course. I spent $536 on newspaper ads that brought 26 calls. The important thing to recognize here is that I said calls, not attendees.

Your Niche

Next, I offered one free workshop through a bookstore, without any paid advertising. The free workshop brought twenty-four **attendees, not calls**. I got hundreds and hundreds of dollars worth of exposure to new prospects in one fun session. That first workshop created new friendships and business relationships that are still active today—years later. Of course, once I had their names and addresses, I never let go of them. I have made it a point to save every name and address, putting it on my mailing list for frequent contact through my newsletter and promotional mailings.

For fun in my marketing workshops, I have a favorite exercise I use to demonstrate why you should do some free community education workshops to get started.

I explain that I'm going to do an exercise to demonstrate why you should do some free workshops to get your practice or business off to a good start.

First, I have everyone take all their change out of their purses or pockets and hold it in their hands. Then, I tell them that when I say "start," I want them to begin giving away some of their money to everyone in the room. Just give out their money; giving some to everyone. I tell them to start and demonstrate by giving some of my money to the closest persons to me. I keep encouraging them to give away their money. As they begin, they start laughing as they get the hang of it. It picks up momentum and becomes a lot of fun. Everyone will be getting money back as quickly as they give it away. The point being that when you **give** you will receive.

Allow this to go on for only a few short minutes. (It's best to stop them while the exercise is at its peak of fun.) Then tell them to spend the next few minutes **getting** as much money from each other as they can, with the object being to see how much they can get. Most people immediately close their hands. They'll immediately see how hard it is to **get** money compared to when they are giving.

This exercise is great fun for a group and serves as a great warm-up too.

Free workshops are a great way to get over stage fright. The people that attend a free workshop all want you to succeed. It's like having your personal rooting section. They appreciate what they're getting for free and bring a nice attitude of expectancy with them. You'll find them to always be most receptive and appreciative of what you present to them.

An added bonus is that your attitude changes from: "I can't speak to all those people," to "Great! Look at how many people my marketing effort has produced." You'll instantly change your attitude from fear of numbers to eager anticipation of greater numbers. When you get five people for your first event, you can't help but being thrilled at your next event when you get ten. After you've gotten ten, you'll be thrilled to get fifteen, and so on. Before you know it, you'll wonder what it was you were fearful of in the first place.

One more thing before we move ahead: When planning an event, always plan a second one at the same time. You're soon going to find out how much effort you have to expend to get your attendees for the first event. Now, while you have all those live, breathing, interested bodies in your presence, is the time to invite them to your next event (even if it's not prepared yet). These are some of your very best prospects for it. You don't even have to spend money for printing or postage to promote it to them. Wouldn't it be cost effective to personally invite all of them? I always do this because I know this kind of marketing effort is going directly to my best prospects—and it costs nothing.

> *"The secret of getting ahead is getting started. The secret of getting ahead is breaking your complex overwhelming tasks into small manageable tasks, and then starting on the first one."*
> *Mark Twain*

Planning Your Workshop or Seminar

No matter what your business, or what type of practice you have, planning your workshop or seminar can follow the same simple procedure.

When I first wanted to put a program together, I sat and stared at my notepad with pen in hand for a long time. Unfortunately, nothing came to mind that satisfied me—so I did nothing. I put the pad aside and let it lay there for days. Later, after mustering up the self-discipline, I sat down with my notepad again. Frustrated an hour later, I had to set it aside again. Was this the "writer's block" I heard so much about? How could it be a block—I hadn't even started. I could not think of how or where to start.

Sometime in the following days as I was driving, I had a thought that could have been at least a start. Unfortunately, the next time I attempted to sit down to my notepad the

Your Niche

thought wouldn't come to me. I then realized that I was not cut out for this. The solution? Find a way—I wanted to do it … period.

Back to my Focused Concentration. It amazed me again— the answer came. *I shouldn't try to sit down to write. Instead, I just needed to make a lot of little notes as thoughts came to me; then save the notes and let them accumulate until I have enough to get started.*

Magic!

It worked!

I still use this simple system today. Even this book began this way, and my other books are in process using this same system.

This is truly not very sophisticated, but if you follow it faithfully, it will get you on your way immediately. You will amaze yourself at just how good you can be.

Keep a small notepad handy everywhere you go. Every time you have a thought or an idea about your topic—jot a note about it.

Every time you see something on a billboard that stirs a thought—jot a note about it.

Every time you hear something of value on the radio—jot a note about it.

Every time you see something of value on TV—jot a note about it.

Your Niche

Watch your junk mail, your newspapers, your magazines, and everything that passes through your hands—if it can be used, cut it out and put it with your notes. By now you should have a folder or shoebox that will soon be full of clippings and notes that all pertain to your topic.

I start several projects at a time like this, and keep file folders on several topics that I might like to do something with some day. So I'm always cutting, jotting, clipping, and filing away tidbits that will become a project some day. Whenever I'm ready—presto! I've got a whole pile of info at hand.

I once thought I'd like to do a class on stress release or stress reduction. I began to keep my eyes open for anything related to stress. Soon my files became so big that I had to move them into a large brown grocery bag. It wasn't long after that that I had to move them into a cardboard box. I never did put together a stress reduction workshop because I never had the time. But I have a box in my attic that has an incredible amount of data ready to be used if I am ever asked to do a presentation or ever decide it's time to do one. I had so much information that I finally stopped saving it.

When you're finally ready to get to work on your presentation, the next step is to empty your files or box of notes onto either a very large table or the floor. Spread your notes and clippings out and sort them into three piles: those that belong in the beginning, the middle, and the end.

Once your notes are organized into three piles, it then becomes easier to arrange them into a pattern that begins to have an organized flow to it. Keep rearranging them until you're satisfied with the order; then tape them together so they become a list. You now have one list for the beginning, one for the middle, and one list for the end.

Your Niche

Now it's time to pull it all together. Start writing from your taped notes. If you can't think of anything to say about a particular item, put it down anyway; you can come back to it later as things start to shape up. Basically what you're doing is using your notes and clippings as springboards for your thoughts. As you move down your taped list, you can write whatever is needed to fill in the blanks and add your thoughts to it. Sometimes I just make up a list of points or an outline for a presentation. As I do the presentation, I make notes in my outline to make additions or changes later.

Immediately after my presentation, I get back into my notes and hold a kind of personal debriefing; adding and changing things while they're fresh in my mind. Today, with computers, this has become incredibly easy to do. You'll find that as time passes and you do your presentation over and over, it will automatically grow and become more comprehensive. That's because you'll have developed the habit of watching for information that relates well to your topic. It's up to you. You can stop its growth by not adding to it, but if you're like me, you'll not be able to resist the opportunity to keep improving and expanding what you've already done.

That's how *your* book is born.

This method, if done as I've described it, will create an outline for any topic and a start for your book with so little effort that it will seem as though it just evolved of itself.

I've found only two difficult things about writing:

1. Getting started.

2. Keeping at it.

Your Niche

After that, the rest is easy.

> *"You don't have to be great to start, but you have to start to be great."*
>
> *Joe Sabal*
> *Professional Speaker*

CHAPTER TWELVE

Location, Location, Location

Don't wait until your program is all prepared to begin looking for a location to present it. You should be thinking about this over a period of time while you're preparing your program. Don't do a presentation in a place merely because it's offered and you can easily arrange it. If you've invested adequate time in preparing the presentation, why waste it on a place that's less than deserving of the fruits of your labors? Look for a place that will benefit you.

You may find a compatible business that complements what you do in a way that will bring you a good audience. This is great because you will then gain many new names for your mailing list by having the attendees sign in, or give you their names for something that you'll offer to send them. (If I'm not passing around a sign-in sheet, I like to have something that they'll want that's not included in my handouts. That way they'll be happy to give me their address.)

I started doing this when one of the bookstore owners I was doing a presentation for objected to my having a sign-in sheet. She didn't want me making a mailing list of her customers. So instead of giving out all my handouts, I held one back. I described one of the choicest handouts and told the attendees I would be happy to mail it to them free of charge—they just had to be sure to tell me where to send it before I left.

Could I refuse to send it to them? Of course not—now I had my addresses.

Keep your eyes open and your creative right brain alert. There are literally a multitude of locations you can use to present your program. I'll list a few examples here just to get you started thinking of the possibilities.

Possible Locations for Free Community Education Workshops or Seminars

❖ Bookstore—The major bookstores are now open to even non-author speakers.

❖ Health club—The competitive market has made them search for items of interest for their members.

❖ Health food store—Again, competition has helped to open the doors to guest speakers.

Location, Location, Location

❖ Park district facility—Most larger cities have an adult education program.

❖ Hotel meeting room—(Always carry your own sound system. Many good seminars have been spoiled by a hotel's bad system.)

❖ Church—With an appropriate topic, you can do a church fundraiser.

❖ Libraries—Most libraries will be open to a community education seminar or workshop if it's free.

❖ Chamber of Commerce—They can line you up with meetings where speakers are wanted.

❖ Radio and TV talk shows—This can be a great opportunity if you write and offer to be an emergency fill-in for them. Send them a list of frequently asked questions so their work will already be done for them and you'll be up on what they'll ask. The odds are in your favor that your day will come—be prepared.

❖ Home seminar—why not? You can send out announcement/invitations. Tell them a guest will be hypnotized, massaged or given a free _____, (whatever your service or product is); receive a valuable free gift, or even a gift discount for each attendee. It can be a relaxed, informal workshop.

I recently saw a segment on a TV news show where a plastic surgeon was conducting home parties giving a slide presentation and answering questions for guests; thereby introducing them to plastic surgery. He was successful because people enjoyed getting the information in such a relaxed, informal atmosphere.

Special note:

Whether conducting a seminar in a hotel, a home, or a meeting place, you're on stage full time. Not only do you have an estimated three seconds to make a first impression, you're being watched and opinions are formed about you. Even if you walk into a public restroom, someone may hear your conversation.

For that reason, you must always remain aware that people are focusing their attention on you even when you're not in the front of the room. One simple remark could easily compromise your credibility.

I once was attending a national convention for a nutritional company. Their whole theme was health and natural living. The CEO for this company consistently drove home the virtues of detoxifying our bodies and only eating pure foods and consuming the best vitamins. You can imagine how fast word traveled around the convention that someone was walking past his hotel suite as the door swung open, accidentally displaying his wife sitting on the bed with a cigarette dangling from her mouth.

On another occasion, an executive from the same company who was always presented as "Mr. Personality," was arriving at the airport for another convention and was spotted at the baggage carousel with his wife. The person that spotted him began to approach him to say hello just as the exec's wife dropped a suitcase that she was loading on the luggage cart. His resulting diatribe of demeaning four letter words directed at his wife was enough to send the greeter not only recoiling from him, but hustling off to the convention to tell everyone what an ogre he was. That story traveled just as fast as the one about the CEO's wife who was caught smoking.

Location, Location, Location

Both of those unfortunate discoveries created an aura of disappointment and suspicion among the people that had previously held these people in high esteem.

Your Attire Sets the Pace

Your attire sets people's opinion of you—and don't think for a moment that it doesn't. The trend today is to dress down. However, I believe that the dress code is still determined at an unconscious level from the top down—not from the bottom up. I think there's a major misconception that has somehow gained momentum even though it's a gross error. I believe the true change is that upper management and the very successful have become more tolerant of those that do not dress for success.

Those who dress for success are doing just that—dressing for success. Being well dressed makes an even greater impression today, because so few do it.

Sure, an earring and/or ponytail for men is acceptable today, but that does not mean they share an equal opportunity to get the business or sale with the person more formally dressed for business. Now there are always exceptions. So, if your business is a guitar store, an art studio, tattoo parlor, or surfboard shop, you can probably set these last remarks aside.

I know a woman who has a doctorate degree and attends conventions and events wearing the same sweatshirt and jeans year after year. If she knew the real opinion others have of her, she'd opt for a more appropriate costume. Yes, she's making a statement all right, but I suspect it's not what she thinks it is. Some people may think that it's quite all right, but I know its seriously hurt her career—people won't refer business to her because they feel it may reflect badly on them.

Promoting Your Seminar/Workshop

Again, you can spend dollars or spend energy—your choice; whichever you have more of. One of my students gave me her fliers and asked me to distribute them for her at a professional chapter meeting every month—they didn't do anything for her. She limited the energy she spent. People wanted to know who she was; they wanted to meet her in person—not receive her fliers from me. She needed to commit *herself* to her marketing effort.

She's back to "sharpening her pencil" again. Pencil sharpening is a term I use to describe those who don't quite get it. They don't succeed for many reasons (usually fear), but instead of finding out or facing those reasons, they go back to school to learn more. They convince themselves that they're not quite ready to get started yet. In the meantime, classmates of theirs have an operating practice or business already up and running.

The best way to get started is to start. Whether you're presenting a free community education program or charging a fee, you have to start establishing yourself as an authority somewhere. There's only one first time—once you have that behind you, you'll have learned things nobody can teach you. Until you have learned those things, you cannot grow into the next steps.

I'm repeating several marketing elements here as a handy guide to promoting your programs:

- Inexpensive three-up fliers—this simple yet effective way to promote your event is bound to produce results. It has never failed and is probably one of the most economical ways to get the word out to a targeted group. If your budget is extremely limited, you can print these on a sheet of 8½ x 11 paper turned sideways and have them copied at your local office supply super store. Then cut them into three fliers to each sheet. Since this plain white paper is not very eye-catching, take a set of colored highlighters and swipe a little rainbow across one corner. You'll be amazed at how well that perks up a flier. Of course, if you own a computer and color printer, you can make this into easy work.

- Inexpensive posters—You can take a full sized 8 ½ x 11 sheet and lay out your posters on fancy preprinted paper, or go right back to highlighting them on a corner. You can put little tabs on the bottom with your phone number. If you do that, tear off the first two tabs. You'll find that that works like priming a pump. No one wants to take a phone number if no one else thinks it's a good idea.

- Get creative/place everywhere—this is a time to again use your right brain. Think of all the places that are frequented by the type of people that are your best prospects. These are the places you want your fliers, and if you're lucky enough to get posters up, all the better. I usually didn't put out brochures for a couple of reasons. The first reason being that they're more expensive. Also, I don't think people on the run will pick up a text-heavy piece of literature. If I can capture their interest in a flier or with a poster, I'll mail them a detailed brochure when they call.

- Set up a route—I never put out a large number of fliers at one place. This only exposes you to having them become messy or risking someone throwing out a large supply. Instead, I put out a conservative amount at each location, and then set up a route for myself. I ran my little route once a week replenishing the supply at each location.

What To Expect From Ads

Don't expect to make money from your ads—you probably won't. Then what are their value? At best, you'll begin building your mailing list. Remember that $536 worth of advertising brought only 26 calls. And that's still only calls—not clients or attendees. It's far better to use your energy by creating fliers, posters, and press releases. I know one therapist that tried just one big ad and was so disappointed when he didn't get any calls, he dropped out. He would never consider spending money on a workshop or a book like this. Why should he pay money for something he can do himself?

What's the value of doing a free workshop? It's an opportunity to add to your mailing list of interested persons. Can building your list be worth working for free? Remember the formula: $536/26 CALLS (not clients) equaled $20.61 per call. This means each name I add to my list is worth over $20.00 in advertising.

CHAPTER THIRTEEN

Presenting The
Seminar/Workshop

• Your Arrival

Be sure to arrive early or you won't get set up on
time. The "eager beavers" also get there early and
want a lot of attention. You'll have a hard time
getting set up because of all the questions they have

and stories they want to tell you, and you'll be frazzled before you get started. Better to beat the eager beavers there, so when they arrive you can spend time with them. The attention you give them is how they will evaluate you and your sincerity. Eager beavers always turn out to be some of your best customers/clients, and you don't want to neglect them. You'll find that in short order you'll have your own following who will not only attend every presentation you offer, they'll bring friends.

• Music

If it's appropriate, have upbeat music playing a little loudly in the background before your session starts. It livens up the group and generates a nice energy. I've experimented with this. I found that if you start out with the music just a little on the loud side and gradually creep the volume up as more people arrive, you'll find your group will be very lively and more fun to work with. Of course, you'll have to use a little caution here as there definitely is a point where you can set it too loud and annoy people.

• Handouts — People like to get "stuff"

People really enjoy receiving reports, notes, and additional information about your topic to take home with them. Do not give out handouts during your presentation. You'll lose the attention of the group, as many of them will invariably begin reading immediately. It's annoying to have to pass them out during your presentation, but it's the only way to keep their attention.

It's best, unless they need to refer to the handouts as part of your presentation, to give them out at the end of the event. This is also an opportunity to offer something else of value that you haven't brought with you. As I said earlier, this is a good way to get names and addresses if you're not able to collect them at the door. Simply offer to mail something to those that are interested.

In your presentation, be sure to give your attendees something of value that they can use. Be sure your presentation does not contain a sales pitch for what you **can, or will** give them if they become a client. A caring useful presentation will produce much more than one that contains a veiled sales pitch. People can be very sensitive to solicitation when they were given to believe they were being offered some valuable information, and then they're "pitched." I once attended a workshop where most of the attendees walked out as the speaker became embroiled in defending herself after a guest loudly complained about her pitching them rather than
giving a genuine seminar.

People don't care how much you know, until they know how much you care.

• Taping

Many seminars, if sponsored by an organization or at a convention, are videotaped or recorded. Always be sure to mention your name and phone number somewhere in the middle of your presentation. That way as the tapes passed around and played, listeners will know who is speaking and how to get a hold of you. Say your name and address in the middle, not the end. That way, when someone copies it, it will be too much trouble to go to the middle to delete it. Every time your presentation is sold, given away, or copied, it is a recorded commercial or infomercial for you.

Another opportunity that may present itself is an invitation for an interview on a local TV cable station. Once you do the interview, you've earned bragging rights to make the all impressive "As seen on TV" claim. It also gives you a chance to get a master video of the program, which you can copy and use as a promotional item. You first should have the cable station agree to give you a ¾ inch master, and permission to copy the program for your own use. Be sure you have this arranged before shooting the show. Also ask if they want you to buy a blank ¾ inch cassette. You'll find that stations often don't have one on hand. At one time I shopped prices to have my own video production taped for marketing purposes. The proposal was for twenty thousand dollars for a twenty-minute video. By speaking for free and arranging for a master, I now have two videos for free, saving over forty thousand dollars.

• Fun

*"The supreme accomplishment is to
blur the line between work and play."
Arnold Toynbee (1889—1975)
Historian*

People want to have fun. They love stories, jokes, activities, and exercises—sometimes so much so that they enjoy it more than learning.

I've been to seminars and workshops where the content was so weak I was sorely disappointed; yet, I've been amazed as I listened for the comments of the attendees as they broke for lunch. They believed they were getting "so much" out of the presentation because the presenter was entertaining. It baffled me that they were satisfied, but there's no denying the fact—they were indeed pleased.

I'm not suggesting that you go light on content and heavy on fun. I don't think that that's very worthwhile for the long haul. However, it's certainly worth keeping in mind the fact that people want to have fun. Always put a little fun in your presentation.

• Your Time

As I said earlier—and it's important enough to repeat: discipline yourself to make it a routine to do your prospecting, whether it's mail or phone calls, first every day. If that's not practical, schedule a certain time each day that, without fail, you will do some business building, and prospecting work.

"Time flies. It's up to you to be the navigator."
Robert Orben
Comedy Writer

If you don't set **rigid rules** for yourself, you'll always find things that need to be done first, and often not get to your prospecting at all.

"The reason most major goals are not achieved is that we spend our time doing second things first.
Robert J. Mckain
Writer

Presenting The Seminar/Workshop

To be efficient and known as reliable, you need a daily "To Do" sheet. You should review and update it nightly so the next day you're off to a productive start. If you do this faithfully, you'll add greatly to your production.

A good way to prioritize the items on your list is with an X or asterisk, or an asterisk in a circle.

When you have an item on your list that is somewhat important, you put an X on it. If an item is more important, you put a line through the X making it into an asterisk. If it is a "must do," you put a circle around the asterisk. This way, you can take an X item and easily upgrade it's importance by adding a line or circle.

Many people work without a daily To Do list. I find they're rarely very efficient—or they never take on much. A successful entrepreneur (and that's certainly what you must be to build a practice or business) must be able to handle a multitude of tasks simultaneously. Multi-tasking eventually becomes second nature but must follow a plan. That plan is best reviewed every night for three reasons: it's a great way to shut your mind off; with everything on paper you won't likely lay in bed awake at night rehearsing the next day's mental To Do list; and, your next day begins with a productive start because you'll be prepared mentally to do the first things first.

"It wasn't raining when Noah built the ark."

Howard Ruff
Writer

• Your Confidence

Confidence comes from adequate preparation. Use Focused Concentration to visualize yourself presenting your entire program. Your subconscious will then be familiar with the presentation, and you'll be more relaxed, more confident, and it will run more smoothly. It will seem as though you've done it all before.

CHAPTER FOURTEEN

Creating The Aura Of Expectancy

You must create an aura of expectancy in every prospective client. The aura of expectancy is the strong belief that you will help them. This can occur automatically with many clients, but when it doesn't occur, you either do not get an appointment or you have a no-show. Rather than wait for the occasions when this aura automatically occurs, you dramatically enhance your business by creating it tactfully.

Creating The Aura Of Expectancy

The creation of the aura begins at the first impression. That can be an ad, your business card, a flier, brochure, or whatever happens to be the prospect's first exposure to you. That means that every marketing piece you produce is very important, as well as the impression a prospective client gets from a phone call to your office. Of course, the best first impression one can get is a personal referral. Nothing creates an aura of expectancy better than a referral.

This means your business card must be professional and not be cluttered with information that looks like you're desperately trying to sell everything you offer on a two-inch by three-inch space. Listing only a P.O. box on your card looks amateur or part time, and clever or cute statements may detract from your professionalism.

If you have a phone directory ad, it must be tasteful and professional—not begging in tone. And the way your calls are answered is very important too. Do not use an answering machine that takes personal calls and business calls on the same number. Today, with cell phones, it's easy to have a separate number with voice mail. You can even use a cell phone in a shared office space without having a phone installed. What could be simpler or more cost effective?

The next step in establishing an aura of expectancy is the way you handle incoming calls. Like anything else, your skill in doing this will improve as you go along. Critique yourself after each call to determine your progress. Don't be too quick to critique the callers that don't make an appointment to see you. The fact always remains, that no matter who the caller is, or what they called for, if they don't set an appointment it is still *you* that didn't create the expectancy. But don't be too critical of yourself. Some callers only want information and you won't be able to turn them around no matter how you handle the call. With experience and the proper handling, your average bookings per call will improve.

I'll explain what I do as a hypnotherapist, and you'll be able to make the necessary adjustments to suit your situation.

Your Three Week Vacation Starts Now

When I started my practice I needed a baseline as a starting point of reference. To begin, I researched the rates in my area and found the midpoint on hypnotherapy rates was eighty-five dollars. That's where I started. As I got calls I immediately accommodated the callers with an appointment within the next few days. From those earliest appointments I got a few no-shows. Once I had my fill of that, I knew I had to enhance the prospective client's perception of value for my services.

How would I do that? I looked at other businesses, both services and products. I saw that very often a higher price enhanced the customers' perception of value—I raised my rates to one hundred and twenty-five dollars. My observations showed that scarcity of an item also enhanced its perception of value in a prospect's eyes. So, I took a three-week vacation and only gave callers appointments three weeks from the time they called. No appointments were set earlier than three weeks after their request. Those two steps alone ended my no-show problem.

To formalize the appointment, I began sending confirmation letters like the following:

Creating The Aura Of Expectancy

Dear John:

This will confirm our first appointment at 5:00 PM, May 4, at the Leidecker Center in Elgin. Please fill out the enclosed forms and return them or fax them back as soon as possible; this will free up some time and afford us the opportunity to accomplish more during your session.

Each session is $125.00. The first session generally lasts one and a half hours at no additional charge; sessions thereafter are one hour. Please refrain from using caffeine a minimum of four hours before your appointment.

Also, please try to arrive promptly at your scheduled time as I may have other clients scheduled immediately following your session.

I look forward to seeing you on the 4th.

Sincerely,
Arthur A. Leidecker, BCH

The day before a new client's first appointment, my office staff makes a confirming call. I've heard one school of thought that you should never make a confirming call because it gives the client an opportunity to cancel. I have never had this happen. In the first place, if everything is handled as professionally as I've described, the clients respect the commitment they've made. Secondly, if they're so irresponsible that they'll use your confirmation call to cancel, they probably weren't planning on showing anyway.

The three week delay in appointments and the increased fee dramatically improved things. The following steps took the situation a step further in improving my practice: I anticipated that a few people might balk at my fee when after

Creating The Aura Of Expectancy

a few increases, at $125.00 it became the highest in my area. Whenever a caller asked about my fee, I told them the amount and then immediately, before they could totally form an objection in their mind, I would say, "The fee is $125.00 per hour but there is no charge for the first half hour consultation." This way, the objection they may be formulating is interrupted by a new thought—the free consultation.

In addition to not being able to get an appointment for at least three weeks, they were paying the highest fees in the area. Now, in addition to that, I won't see any clients for less than three sessions. Before they can fully formulate a question or objection to that factor, I can immediately say it this way: "I only see clients for a minimum of three sessions because I teach you self-hypnosis so you can reinforce the work we do, and handle any future challenges in your life without the need for additional help."

You must explain these statements pretty closely as I have described, because what you are doing is anticipating objections and intercepting the full development of them in the client's mind with the description of a positive benefit.

All of this is truly to the client's benefit because I can certainly do much more for them in three sessions than I can ever do in only one.

I'm entitled to the highest fee in my area because I put more effort and planning in helping every client that sees me.

The benefit to me, of course, is that instead of one appointment, each client sees me for a minimum of three. This gives me an overlap of clients and levels out my income flow. It takes far too much effort and/or expense to see a new client only one time. If that's your practice, either you won't last or you will certainly live a poor existence.

If I were a chiropractor, Reiki practitioner, lawn care specialist, massage specialist, or a personal exercise trainer, it would make no difference. I can always find good, legitimate reasons why more than one visit or appointment is better.

You must create ways that more visits or sessions are better, and then you must know it and believe it. Think of ways you can add value to what you do for clients so that they will want to avail themselves of your additional sessions or visits.

After applying all the techniques necessary to obtain clients or customers, there's a lot you can do to make sure you make the sale. There are seven channels of non-verbal communication. The entire subject is far too vast to cover in this book, but I'll give you some of the information here so you'll be able to put it to work. Using the seven channels together gives you an incredible insight into what your prospective client or customer is thinking. In fact, if they're not giving you strong enough signals, there are tests you can perform that will tell you how to proceed with them. Any top-notch salesman will tell you that knowing when to close the sale, and when to close your mouth, is a critical part of every sale.

Dr. Edward T. Hall, professor of anthropology at Northwestern University, coined the word *proxemics*. Proxemics is the way others and we manage space as it relates to us personally. Used in combination with the other channels of communication, it strengthens your mastery of managing situations.

Creating The Aura Of Expectancy

Imagine yourself walking into a doctor's waiting room. At the far end of a row of chairs a woman, the only other person in the room, is sitting closest to the receptionist's window. Upon signing in with the receptionist, where are you expected to sit? What would occur if you were to sit right next to the woman? Most likely she would get up, go to the ladies room, and/or walk over to the magazines, select one and casually (she may even browse pictures on the wall first) sit down further away from you.

Now if you sat at the opposite end of the row of chairs where you were expected to sit, where would the third person coming into the room sit—right in the middle of course. Now a fourth person comes in and he gets two choices—in the middle, between the center person and either end person. I don't need to go on, because you already can picture the fifth person walking in and sitting down.

Even though our "personal space" is adjusted culturally around the world, we all have an unspoken appropriate personal space that we unconsciously want people to respect. Any crowding of that space is considered an intrusion. Europeans tend to allow the space to be a little closer than in the U.S. In the Middle East that space is much closer.

It seems to be related directly to the density of the population of the region or country. Up in rural, northern Wisconsin, often when I walked up to someone and held out my hand in a gesture to greet them with a handshake, they would look down at my hand as if they wondered why I was sticking my hand into their personal space.

I've traveled all over the world doing research for my book on Neuro-subliminal Communication™. I found great differences from country to country in how personal space is managed. In Beijing, China, it's so congested that their personal space is very small. Even in their tiny, crowded homes, a person's personal space may be limited to the spot where they keep their neatly folded change of clothes and other possessions. It's no wonder in a country that's barely a sliver bigger than the U.S., yet has a billion more people (this is worth pondering).

They don't cue-up in lines. It's apparently hopeless. They just merge forward constantly pushing ahead. At night in the very dimly lit streets, the silent mass of bicycles is moving all night long. Rush hour is forever—even at 3:00 AM. The streets below the window of my hotel were seething with people. Yet after spending nine days with my Chinese guide, with whom I became very close friends, when I stepped into her very tiny private space to hug her goodbye, she turned to stone and was obviously uncomfortable. The perimeter of her space was very small, and very private.

In Tangiers, Morocco, the street vendors use intrusion into your personal space to intimidate you into buying their wares. They get into your space and don't back off until either you buy something or you push them away. In one instance, a street vendor selling daggers crowded into my space in such an imposing way, that it was hard to determine if he was crossing the fine line of showing me his dagger, or attempting a robbery at knife point.

In Egypt, however, the young boys selling items to the tourists use proxemics in a more clever way. They get very close to you and in a gentle voice coax you to take what they're selling in your hand. Once you do, you practically own it, because they immediately step out of your space so you must make an effort (usually a few steps) to give it back to them. This movement is very subtle, and before you know it, space has been manipulated. You're unconsciously tempted to just buy it rather than to try to give it back to them. They've even taken it a step further. If you do resist the unconscious nudge to just buy it, when you try to return it to them they say, "No keep it. It's a gift." Why not make it awkward for you? Usually the item is only a dollar U.S. So you'll end up giving them the money anyway. This obviously works well with them or they wouldn't keep doing it.

In Istanbul, Turkey, the Kurdish children approach you using proxemics as they step into your space in a non-threatening way. Then, using touch, they get very close and lightly hold your hand. Before you realize what's happening, they use kinesics and make eye contact with you with the deepest, darkest, most engaging eyes you've ever seen, and try to sell you a small package of facial tissue for twenty-five cents. No one, but no one, only gives them a quarter. Once they get your dollar they thank you, kiss the dollar, and immediately take your hand again to walk with you a little way. How many people can resist the urge to give their newfound little friend a little something extra?

Obviously none of these children have had any formal training, but as the saying goes, "Necessity is the mother of invention."

In Israel the pickpockets used proxemics and touch on their victims at a time when their guard is down. I was present when four tourists quickly had their pockets and belt pouches emptied almost simultaneously.

Several elderly tourists had mistakenly felt secure as they cued-up to re-board their tour bus after a hectic tour through the winding, crowded, narrow streets of old Jerusalem. Just as they were about to step up into the bus, one man of the pickpocket team stepped right into their space, preventing them from boarding, on the pretense of a last minute attempt to show and sell them postcards. In the midst of this rude intrusion of their space, his partner, also holding up a handful of postcards, touched them in several places using touch as a method of kinesthetic disorientation. In the midst of all this confusion, a third "postcard seller" helped himself. The amazing thing is that none of the victims were aware of the thefts until the bus was on its way. They were too preoccupied with the rudeness of their space being violated and all the touching and bumping.

While this discussion is about proxemics, the management of space, it is essential that you also understand kinesics (body, or muscle movement). The muscle movement in kinesics is the important signal that tells you a person is adjusting their personal space. Sometimes this movement is very subtle, and before you know it space has been manipulated—and quite possibly, you along with it. Kinesics also includes the movement of eyes, which when combined with the other channels, can be very communicative.

Shortly after playing host in the U.S to my gypsy friend and just before sending him home, I became aware that I was somehow always picking up the check for meals in restaurants. I had never really thought about it much until one day when I had an opportunity to watch him in action. Three of us had been sitting in a booth having lunch. He was sitting directly across from me. To my right, at the end of the table, were the salt and peppershaker, a catsup bottle, and a chrome napkin dispenser. Our sandwiches had been served with French fries on waxed paper in those oval plastic baskets that you've most likely seen in restaurants. The baskets were still setting empty in front of each of us. Our waitress approached with the check and placed it on edge between the catsup bottle and the napkin dispenser. She walked away and we continued speaking.

Creating The Aura Of Expectancy

What happened next explained how I somehow always ended up with the check. Very slowly, very casually, yet very deliberately, my friend started moving his oval basket. Every now and then it got a little nudge. Eventually it was nudged enough to "block" him from the check but form a perfect gateway to me. Now if I'm not a person to make a big deal over who picks up the check, this action would be a subliminal suggestion to my subconscious mind to "pick up the check—it's easier for you." This can work even if it only occurs in the periphery of your field of vision. Your subconscious mind also is aware of that which appears only in your peripheral vision. This is why in forensic hypnotism investigators can obtain details from crime scenes that a witness does not know at a conscious level, yet knows subconsciously. Have you ever somehow picked up a check you didn't really want? Will it ever happen to you again?

You can also successfully use proxemics to test your rapport with a person in just about any situation. On any table or desk shared by two people, there's an imaginary line separating your space from theirs. The person across from you will accept a certain amount of intrusion across that imaginary line based on their level of comfort with you, or what you're saying or doing. If they're not comfortable with you or what you're saying, you may notice a slight adjustment of the space between you as they increase the distance.

A car salesman could test his rapport with a prospect by slightly crowding his space in a non-threatening way, and watching for the prospect to subconsciously readjust it. If no readjustment is made, a reasonably good level of rapport is established. If the prospect does readjust the space to its original distance, rapport has not been established and more work has to be done to improve its level.

Creating The Aura Of Expectancy

This test can be also done at the desk with the car purchase agreement. The salesman may casually move the contract on the desk until it crosses the imaginary line. The kinesthetic response of moving back, no matter how slightly, shows subconscious rejection as the proxemics is readjusted. This, of course, establishes that rapport is not yet sufficient to close the sale. On the other hand, if the prospect allows the salesman to move the contract over the line and leans forward, he is showing his eagerness to buy. If the prospect happens to put his hand down and unconsciously touches the contract, there's no need to go any further. Just hand him the pen. He's ready to sign.

A real estate salesperson can easily make any adjustments necessary to create a level of rapport with prospects that will put his competition in the background. Here I'll deal with the use of proxemics and, of course, the accompanying kinesics. Later, in the discussion on posture echoing, I'll add another dimension you can use in conjunction with this already powerful method of testing and creating rapport.

While discussing handling the sale of a client's property, the agent can bring up various issues that must be dealt with, without taking an immediate position until he can determine the client's opinion.

For example: The agent might say, "I'd like to talk to you a little about lockboxes Mr. Smith." At this point the agent carefully observes the client watching for clues. If he doesn't like the use of lockboxes, he may move back slightly. This movement can be subtle and very quick. At this point the agent can say, "In your case Mr. Smith, I'd prefer to not use one so that I can maintain better control over your property." On the other hand, if Mr. Smith leans forward, it's an indication that he likes the idea of a lockbox and the agent can say, "I'd like to put a lockbox on your front door Mr.

Creating The Aura Of Expectancy

Smith, because that way we can be sure to get as many prospective buyers through your home as possible." Either way, the agent can build rapport by watching this kinesthetic management of the proxemics. Since the agent already knows how to determine Mr. Smith's readiness to sign the listing contract, he already knows whether it's time to hand Mr. Smith the pen, or present more benefits before closing the deal.

When showing a property, the same agent can ask his client, "What do you think of this place?" The client may shift his weight away from the agent just a little, or shift his weight away to a leg or foot and the agent then knows he's rejecting the property. If the client likes the property, he may be hesitant to show it for fear of it costing him more. He may, however, show his true feelings in a number of ways: he may lean just a little forward; he may slightly and quickly lick his lips *(a strong positive);* he may touch a finger to his lips *(a stronger positive)*; or may even put a pen to his lips *(a stronger positive yet)*. No matter what the prospect says—he likes the property.

Some of what I've described here is kinesics, because there's usually movement connected to the adjustment of the proxemics, or space. The relationship of one to the other is consistent, but in some instances the movement of something may not occur in your presence. The movement or arrangement of space may have not been done in your presence, but you'll still see the result of it. This could be expressed in the placement of chairs, the placement of food on a table, the placement of furnishings in a home, deck chairs on a cruise ship, and on and on . . . any place where the management of space can take place.

Creating The Aura Of Expectancy

It won't take you long at all to pick up on these movements, now that you're aware of proxemics as a channel of communication. You'll become aware of what's always been going on around you. To accelerate your awareness, I'm suggesting a few fun projects for field research.

While standing next to someone, casually and slowly encroach on their space. You'll know when they've felt it. They'll casually shift their weight away from you. You can also do this test while facing them, but it takes a little nerve on your part.

Next, while sitting at a table with someone, slowly slide items across the imaginary line. Do it casually so it's not obvious. At some point they'll clearly become discomforted by it. They may even lean or push back from the table. If they show no reaction or even lean forward, they may be open to your invasion of their space. Further testing should give the answer.

For the last item of proxemics research, walk into any place where people wait seated in a row and sit next to someone. This will only be revealing if there are plenty of choices of seats available farther away from this person. Usually your sitting next to them will unnerve them. Men can readily experience this phenomenon simply by walking into a large men's restroom where there are several available urinals. If there is only one man standing at a urinal, walk over and use the one next to him. I've never had the nerve to do this myself, but I know without question that he'll lift an eyebrow when you step right next to him. There's an unwritten law that you never use a urinal next to someone unless there's no other choice. In fact, many men will step into a cubicle and use a toilet when there's only one man but too few urinals to use a sufficiently distant one.

Creating The Aura Of Expectancy

If you want to know more, in my book: ***Thanks For Telling Me—The Advanced Technical Science of Body Language***, you'll find over a hundred neuro-subliminal gestures and an entire education that reaches far beyond any studies in body language available.

CHAPTER FIFTEEN

Your Determination To Succeed

"With every disadvantage,
there is always a greater
advantage."
    W. Clement Stone
    Business Executive

Your Determination To Succeed

Along the way remember: There is a counteracting positive to every negative situation that occurs. And it does exist. When you look hard enough you'll find it. I've tested this theory over and over again and it does two things that can change your business life and, quite frankly, your personal life too. Once you've proved that it works for you, you'll have wonderful peace of mind. You'll never see business mishaps in the same unnerving way again. The other benefit is believing this—and looking until you find the positive. Its the key to leaping over roadblocks that repeatedly cause others to stumble.

"Diamonds are nothing more than
chunks of coal that stuck to their job."
Malcolm Forbes (1919—1990)
Publisher

You take advantage of the fact that you might be in different moods from time to time and feel differently about things from one day to the next. The following worksheet helps you track your feelings about what you might do to build your business. Complete it and then you can select the ideas you like best and consider the most promising.

SUCCESS WORKSHEET

Each day for a week write five finishes to this sentence:

If I really wanted to be wealthy I would . . .

_____

_____

_____

_____

_____

_____

_____

If I really wanted to be wealthy I would . . .

_____

_____

_____

_____

_____

_____

_____

If I really wanted to be wealthy I would . . .

_____

_____

_____

_____

Your Determination To Succeed

_____
_____
_____
_____

If I really wanted to be wealthy I would . . .

_____
_____
_____
_____
_____
_____
_____
_____

If I really wanted to be wealthy I would . . .

_____
_____
_____
_____
_____
_____
_____
_____

Your Determination To Succeed

List the three most promising from the above, and **GET STARTED!**

_____

_____

_____

_____

_____

A while back I invited a business acquaintance to join me in exploring a software idea I had, to see if it had any merit as a business opportunity. If it showed any real promise I would be willing to consider working out a partnership arrangement. We embarked on our marketing research and after a time had really gotten only disappointing results. I felt the opportunity was still there, but that a different approach needed to be developed.

My acquaintance apparently saw all the negatives as an indication that the idea just wasn't going to work. After several attempts to meet with him, and no returned calls from my messages wanting to discuss a new strategy, I set out alone. I believed that there was a counteracting positive to the negative response, and that the rejection of the product was a learning step—not failure. I started marketing differently and continued pushing, believing there was an opportunity—not the original one, but a different and better idea that evolved from the first. Instead of marketing software, I started marketing hardware—and giving software away as a premium.

It worked! And you probably guessed it—the acquaintance called almost a year later asking, "Are **we** making any money yet?"

Your Determination To Succeed

"Success seems to be largely a matter of hanging on after others have let go."
William Feather (1889—1981)
Writer and Publisher

You have to know when to push on and when to give up.

The following worksheet will help you lay out a game plan that will be tailor made for you, indicating exactly where you should focus your attention on building your practice in it's appropriate position of priority. Complete the form and prioritize it by following the simple grading formula at the end.

First Things First

On a 1—10 Scale (with 10 being the greatest) Difficulty

		Time To Implement	Time To See Results	Total
___	CSC Compelling Sales Concept	_____	_____	_____
___	Risk Elimination	_____	_____	_____
___	Writing Successful Ads	_____	_____	_____
___	Advertising Idea File	_____	_____	_____
___	Mail Advertising	_____	_____	_____
___	Checklist For Sales Letter Writing	_____	_____	_____
___	Testing	_____	_____	_____
___	Free Advertising	_____	_____	_____

Your Determination To Succeed

___	Almost Free Advertising	_____	_____	_____
___	Writing	_____	_____	_____
___	Seven Second Presentations	_____	_____	_____
___	Fliers, Posters, and Brochures	_____	_____	_____
___	Tear-off Posters	_____	_____	_____
___	Three-up Fliers	_____	_____	_____
___	Host Beneficiary Relationships	_____	_____	_____
___	Referral Programs	_____	_____	_____
___	Six Steps to More Referrals	_____	_____	_____
___	Customer Loyalty	_____	_____	_____

Your Determination To Succeed

____   Regaining
Clients   _____   _____   _____

____   Selling
More   _____   _____   _____

____   Additional
Revenue
Streams   _____   _____   _____

____   Scalloping   _____   _____   _____

____   Your
Niche   _____   _____   _____

____   Building
Your
Practice
with
Seminars   _____   _____   _____

____   Planning
Your
Program   _____   _____   _____

____   Promoting
Your
Seminar/
Workshop   _____   _____   _____

Combine the first and second column. Start your accelerated business building strategy with the item with the lowest combined number first. Next, take the second lowest number and so on until you have checked off each item. You'll

Your Determination To Succeed

notice that as you implement the steps, it will become increasingly difficult to go to the next one because you'll be getting busier in your practice.

The best advice I can give you now is to sit down, complete your *First Things First* worksheet, your *If I Wanted To Be Wealthy I Would*, worksheet and . . . **Get Started.**

> *"There's plenty of time to lay around
> when we're dead."*
> *My Personal Slogan*
> *Arthur A. Leidecker, BCH*
> *Hypnotist and Author*

You Can Learn Neuro-subliminal Communication™

The Advanced Technical Science of Body Language

Discovered through years of worldwide research and developed by Arthur A. Leidecker, BCH.

Contact Art Leidecker
224-805-6661
www.artleidecker.com

Group and corporate courses available throughout the U.S. and worldwide.

Index

Index

Index

Index

Index

Index

Index

Index